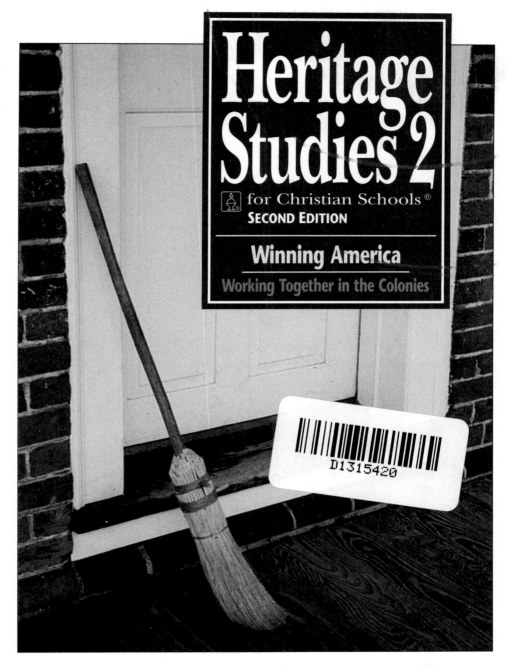

Heritage Studies 2
for Christian Schools®
SECOND EDITION

Winning America

Working Together in the Colonies

Kimberly H. Pascoe and Dawn L. Watkins

Bob Jones University Press, Greenville, South Carolina 29614

HERITAGE STUDIES 2 for Christian Schools®
Making America: Working Together in the Colonies
Second Edition

Kimberly H. Pascoe
Dawn L. Watkins

Produced in cooperation with the Bob Jones University Department of Social Studies Education of the School of Education, the College of Arts and Science, and Bob Jones Elementary School.

for Christian Schools is a registered trademark of Bob Jones University Press.

© 1996, 1998 Bob Jones University Press
Greenville, South Carolina 29614
First Edition © 1981 Bob Jones University Press

Printed in the United States of America
All rights reserved

ISBN 0-89084-885-8

15 14 13 12 11 10 9 8 7 6

Contents

Geography

American History

Government

Economics

World History

Culture

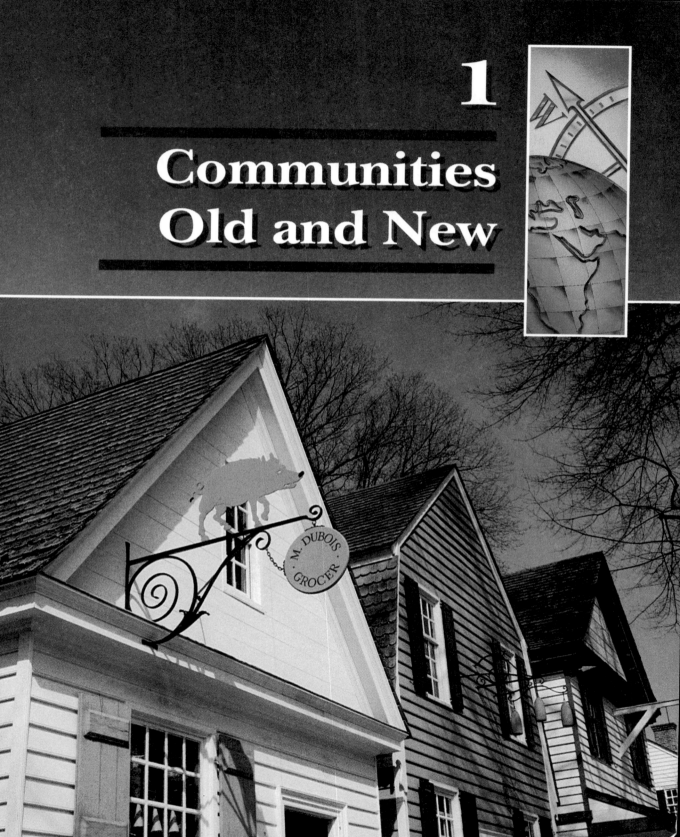

1

Communities Old and New

Your Community

What do you see on your way to school? Do you see lots of houses and other buildings? Do you see pastures and barns? Do you see gas stations and stores? What you see tells you what kind of *community* you live in.

A community is a place where many people live. Some communities are small towns or villages. Some are groups of farms. Some are big cities like Boston or Dallas. Some are *suburbs,* between big cities and small towns or farms.

Most communities have a school and churches and a gas station or some kind of store. Some have their own post offices and fire stations. Many have libraries and hospitals and offices. Which of these things does the town on the map have? What does your community have?

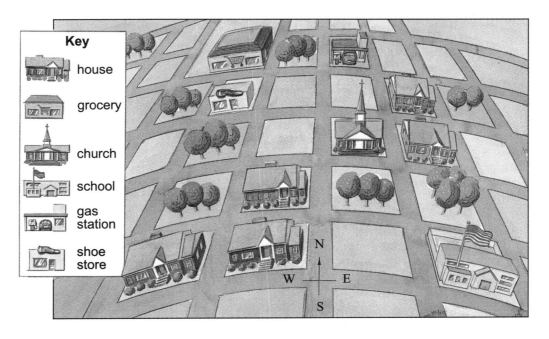

Fire Stations

"Fire! Fire!" A boy ran down a Jamestown street. He called for help. People came out of their houses with buckets and barrels. They made a line down to the river. They began to fill buckets with water and pass them up the line toward the fire.

Do you think the buckets of water stopped many fires in villages long ago? Most often the buildings burned down. Sometimes the whole town burned down. Jamestown burned down eighty years after people first settled there.

Why do you think the towns were always in danger of burning? Many jobs used fire. Bakers baked with fire. Candle makers heated fat with fire. Every house had a fireplace. And most of the houses were made of wood. Why do you think stone houses were built later?

If you saw a fire today, how would you get help? You would not have to run through the streets as the boy in Jamestown did. You would pick up a telephone. Your call would go to a fire station. Then fire engines and firefighters would zoom to the fire.

When the alarm goes off at a fire station, firefighters move fast. They pull on coats and gloves that do not burn. They yank on boots and put on helmets. Why do they wear all these clothes?

The firefighters do not use buckets. They drive huge trucks. They take ladders and axes and gas masks. They use hoses that spray gallons and gallons of water onto the fire. Even big fires can be stopped now.

A Fire Station Works

1. Write to a fire station near your school. Ask the firefighters when you can visit the station.

2. Your teacher will tell you what day your trip to the fire station will be. Think about what questions you would like to ask the firefighters.

3. Visit the fire station. Draw a picture of the most exciting part of your visit. Write a thank-you letter to the firefighters.

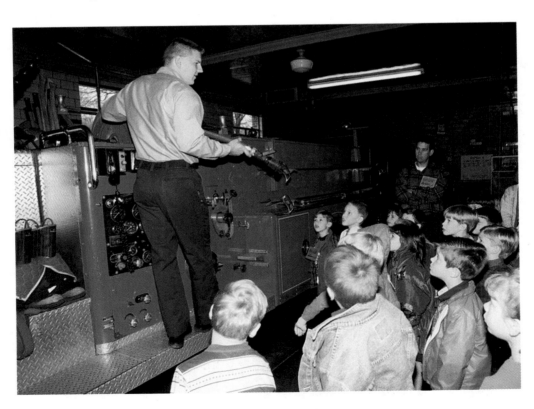

Post Offices

A lady stood near the dock. "Will you please take a letter to my father and mother in England?" The sailor took the letter. He got onto his ship. "I hope I can find her father and mother," he said to himself.

People have always tried to send messages to others. Indians sent messages with smoke. Messengers ran from house to house with notes. And sailors took letters across the water on ships.

Would you like to send a message in one of these ways? A person could not be sure his letter would get to the right place if he sent it with someone else. The letter might be lost. The sailor might forget to deliver it. Can you think of other things that might happen to the letter?

Today we have a better way to send messages. We call the way we send messages the *postal system*. We call the letters and other things we send *mail*. Have you ever sent mail?

We write an *address* on the outside of each piece of mail we send. The address tells where the mail is going. This letter is going to David Nell in Dallas. What happened after Katie mailed the letter?

David got the letter! Whom would you like to get a letter from?

Libraries

Ben Franklin liked to read books. Sometimes he spent all his money on a new book. "We must all put our books together," Ben told his friends. "Then we will all have more books to read. We will have our own library."

Long ago, books cost a lot of money. It was hard to print and bind them. Some books were even written by hand. Only very rich people could buy many books. Most families had only one book. What book do you think that was?

Ben Franklin's library began with only thirty-five books. It was the first *lending library* in his town. A lending library is a place where people can come to look at books. They can even take the books home with them.

To Read a Map Key

1. Get your Notebook and some colored pencils or crayons.

2. Take out the Notebook page your teacher tells you to.

3. Answer the questions your teacher asks by looking at the map and the key. Use the pencils to color the map and the key to match.

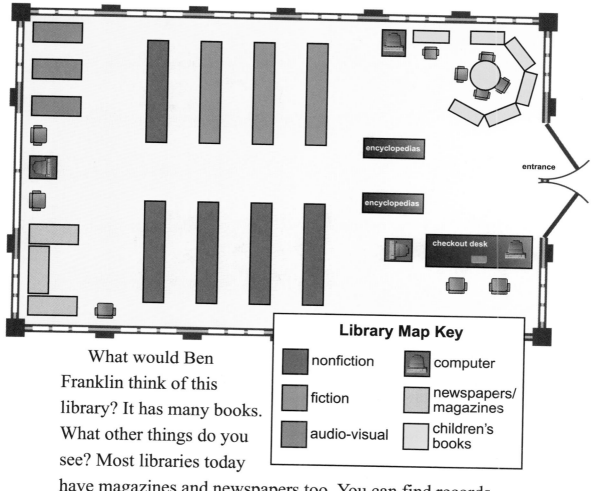

Library Map Key

■ nonfiction		■ computer	
■ fiction		■ newspapers/magazines	
■ audio-visual		■ children's books	

What would Ben Franklin think of this library? It has many books. What other things do you see? Most libraries today have magazines and newspapers too. You can find records, filmstrips, videos, and even toys. What things would you like to look for in a library?

Special people work in a library. Do you know what we call these people? We call them *librarians*. Librarians can help you find the things you want to see. They know where to find the book, record, or magazine that you want. Can you find the checkout desk?

Hospitals

All of a sudden an arrow shot by. A soldier fell down. "I'm hit," he said. His arm was bleeding.

What do you think happened to the soldier then? Long ago, there were no ambulances to pick up hurt people. There were only six or seven places in all the colonies that took care of sick people. And those places also held poor people and orphans and often thieves.

Such places were called *pesthouses*. The hurt soldier would not want to go there. Almost everyone who went there died. He would wait for someone to help him get home. He would pray to get well.

What a shock it would be for the wounded soldier to see a hospital today! Hurt people can be picked up by ambulances or even helicopters. They go to clean, bright emergency rooms to get help.

Hospitals have many doctors and nurses. The doctors have special machines to help them find out what is wrong with sick people. They use x-ray machines, scanners, and equipment that uses sound to look inside the body. Have you ever had an x-ray?

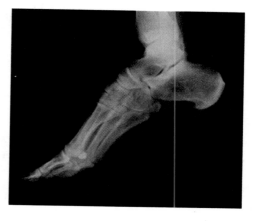

There are some hospitals that are just for children. The walls have pictures on them, and the chairs and beds are the right size. Even children who have to stay in bed can play games and do crafts.

Why do we need fire stations and hospitals? We need them because fires start and people get sick and hurt and need help to get well. We try to keep our cities and towns safe.

God tells us of another kind of city. He tells us that the city of heaven will be perfect. That city needs no fire stations or hospitals. It will last forever.

But now they desire a better country, that is, an heavenly: wherefore God is not ashamed to be called their God: for he hath prepared for them a city.
Hebrews 11:16

Gustave Doré, The Ascension,
The Bob Jones University Collection

2

Farming

On a Farm

Do you live on a farm? Have you ever visited a farm? What do you find on a farm? There are almost always animals and tractors. What else might there be?

What do you think farms were like a long time ago? Once there were no tractors or electric lights in the barns. There were no trucks carrying vegetables and fruit to market. All the work was done by hand while the sun shined.

He that tilleth his land shall be satisfied with bread.

Proverbs 12:11

Old Farms

Farmers in Benjamin Franklin's day had tools different from what farmers use today. Their plow was a wooden blade that cut into the ground. It was usually pulled by a team of oxen. The farmer walked behind the plow to steer it.

Do you think the fields were big or small? The fields were small. After a farmer plowed all day, he was tired. His animals were tired. But there was still work to be done. What do you think had to be done?

The farmer had to feed and water the animals. There were no hoses or faucets in the barns. The farmer carried water in buckets from a stream or well. The farm may have had chickens and pigs as well. What other animals might a farmer have kept?

When the fields were plowed, the farmer planted seeds in them. He walked through the fields. He threw seeds out on the ground. He planted wheat, corn, oats, and other crops.

What do you think happened to the seeds after they were planted?

Some of them grew into plants. Some got washed away by the rains. The birds ate some of them. Farmers' children often sat in the fields to chase birds away. Would you like that job?

What Grew on Farms

What could have happened to the crops that grew? What happened when there was not enough rain? The crops dried up. What happened when there was too much rain? The crops were flooded. What happened when the weather got cold early? The crops did not finish growing. Do you think farmers watched the weather closely?

Look at the map. Where was most of the corn grown? What crops were grown in the South? Farmers in the South grew some crops like cotton and rice. Why do you think the farmers in the North did not grow these crops? The summers are not long enough in the North for these crops. What things does a farmer have to think about when he plants?

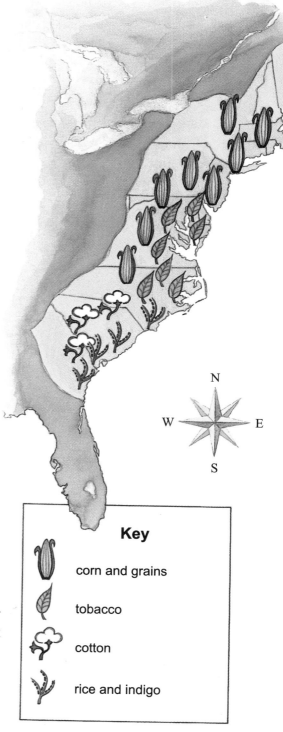

Key

corn and grains

tobacco

cotton

rice and indigo

Look at the picture chart. Which crop grew best? Which crop grew least well? What might have happened to the wheat?

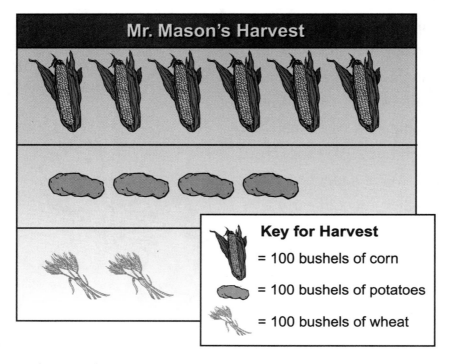

Why was it important that the crops grew well? The farmer and his family needed the crops for food for themselves and for feed for the animals. Without a good harvest, the winter would be hard to live through.

When a crop grew well, the farmer brought it into the barn. He *harvested* it. Do you remember what the people of Plymouth Plantation did when they had a harvest? They thanked God. Our *Thanksgiving Day* began with them. We too should thank the Lord for our blessings.

Grain like wheat has to be cut down to be harvested.
Farmers used a sharp curved blade called a *scythe* to cut down
grain. The farmers walked through the grain. They swung
their scythes as they walked. Whish! went the scythe.
The grain fell. Have you ever seen someone sweeping with a
broom? The farmers with scythes looked something like that.

Farmers also grew other plants and raised animals. They used parts of the plants and animals to make cloth. Cotton plants have fruit that look something like large cotton balls with seeds in them. Farmers would pull the fruit off the plant, take out the seeds, and make cotton thread from the cotton fruit. The threads are made into cloth. Cotton is still used to make cloth. Do you own something made of cotton?

Some people raised sheep. What do we get from sheep? We get wool from sheep. Farmers cut the wool off sheep in the spring. The sheep do not need their wool in the warm weather.

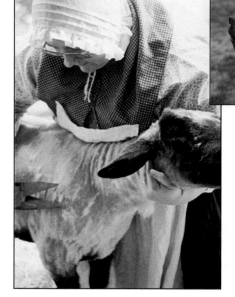

Other people spin the wool into yarn. Then the yarn is made into cloth. Do you have any clothes made of wool?

To Make Cloth

1. Get some wool or cotton yarn. Your teacher will give you a frame.

2. Watch your teacher as she weaves first. Then as she tells you, take your turn adding to the cloth.

3. How long do you think it would take to make enough cloth for a coat?

Elizabeth Lucas Pinckney
(1722-1793)

Colonists made clothes from wool, cotton, and linen. Cotton threads and linen and wool yarns were usually white or off-white. To make them any other color, they had to be *dyed*.

A *dye* is a stain that changes the color of cloth. One of the best dyes is called *indigo*. Indigo makes cloth a dark blue. Indigo was a favorite dye in early America.

A girl named Elizabeth grew indigo plants on her father's farm. The dye sold very well. At sixteen, Elizabeth took over three farms. She taught other people to grow indigo. Soon America began selling much dye to other countries. Why was that important?

Modern Farms

Long ago, farmers kept much of the food they grew. They fed their own families and animals. Sometimes they traded with each other. If a man wanted extra wool, he might trade his neighbor some corn for some wool.

Today farmers grow far more than their families need. A farmer in America can grow enough food for his family and forty other people. Why do you think the farmers can grow so much?

Farmers now have tractors to pull their plows. Do you think plows today look the same as they did in Benjamin Franklin's day? They do not. The plows today can open several rows in the ground at once.

How do you think seeds are planted now? Do you think farmers throw them out by hand? No, there are machines that do the planting. With the help of machines, farmers can plant much more in a day.

Machines also make harvesting faster. Some machines pick corn. Some pick cotton. Some cut wheat. What other machines do you think farmers use?

Look at the graphs on this page. What crops are grown the most on modern farms in one part of our country?

How much more land can a farmer plow with a machine than with horses?

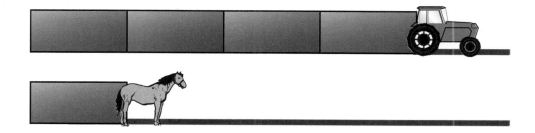

Can you guess what the machine in the picture is doing?
It was invented more than one hundred years ago by Cyrus
McCormick. The machine is cutting grain. McCormick's
machine was improved. Men made it bigger. Soon it was
so big that it took forty horses to pull it.

Now a machine for cutting grain looks like this. How is it different from McCormick's first machine? What makes it go? It has an engine that runs on gasoline.

Farmers have machines that milk cows. Look at the picture graph. How many more cows can this farmer milk in a day by machine than by hand?

Mr. Mason's Milking

Cows milked by machine each day

Cows milked by hand each day

Growing New Plants

Scientists try to grow better plants. Sometimes they try to get tomatoes to be bigger. Sometimes they try to get wheat that can stand more heat. Why do you think people try to make better plants?

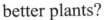

One way to grow better plants is to keep the seeds from the best plants. It is likely that those seeds will grow into stronger plants than the seeds from plants that did not grow as well.

Do you like to grow things?

3

Starting the Colonies

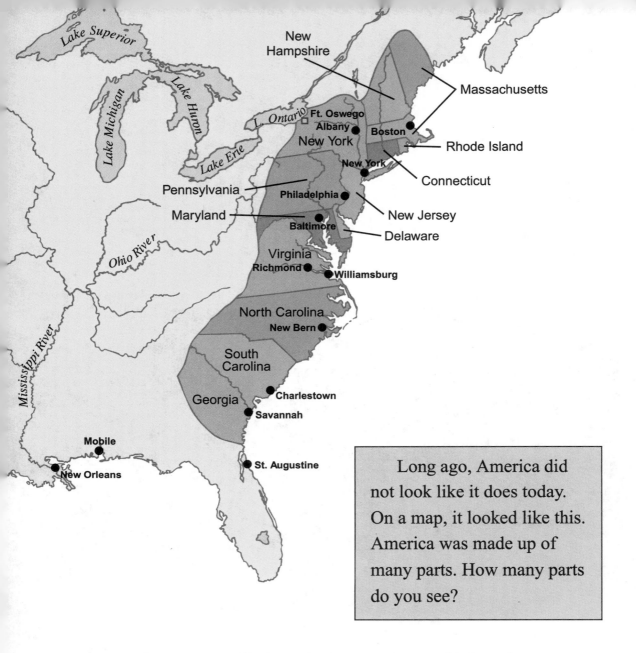

Long ago, America did not look like it does today. On a map, it looked like this. America was made up of many parts. How many parts do you see?

Each part was called a *colony*. How do you think each colony got started? People left their old countries to come to a colony for many reasons. Do you know any of those reasons?

The First English Colony

One hundred five men came to live in the Virginia Colony. They called the place they lived *Jamestown*. The men told each other, "We don't have time to plant gardens and build houses in Jamestown. We must hunt for gold. Finding gold will make us rich."

The men did not find gold. But they did find something that made them rich. They found a plant that the Indians grew. The men planted it in their gardens. They sold the plant to people in England. Do you know what the plant was? It was *tobacco*.

Do you think everyone was happy about the new plant? Some people were not. King James said, "Smoking is harmful to the brain and to the lungs. The smoke makes me think of the pit of Satan." Most men and women did not listen to King James. But today we know that King James was right.

A Trading Post Colony

A few years later, men from another country sailed across the ocean. They sailed north of the Virginia Colony. The men came from the country called the *Netherlands*. Why do you think they came to America? They came to trade with the Indians.

These men called their colony New Netherland. Trading with the Indians made some men rich. What kinds of things do you think they traded? Often the Indians traded piles of furs. The men from the Netherlands traded things like beads, knives, and tools.

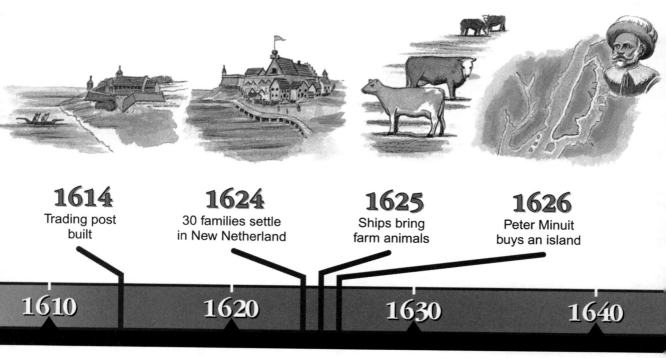

1614
Trading post built

1624
30 families settle in New Netherland

1625
Ships bring farm animals

1626
Peter Minuit buys an island

1610   1620   1630   1640

One man named Peter Minuit made a special trade
with the Indians. He gave the Indians beads, knives, and tools.
But they gave him something much bigger than a pile of furs.
The Indians gave him a whole island! Peter built a town
on the island. He called the town New Amsterdam.

Today, we know New Amsterdam
by a different name. Men from England
changed the name when they came to take
over the colony. The men named it for
their leader, the duke of York. We now call
the town New York City.

1664
English take over
New Netherland

1650   1660

Raising Animals

Have you ever visited a farm? What kinds of animals did you see there? Most farm animals are *tame* animals. Many of them make good pets. Would you like to have one of these animals as a pet?

Most of the animals that the Indians knew about were not tame. These animals lived in the forest. They did not make good pets. The only pets Indians knew about were dogs. They had never seen the animals we can see at a farm.

The settlers had always kept tame animals. They needed them for milk and meat. They needed them for helping on the farm. The settlers wanted to bring animals with them. Four ships came to New Amsterdam with animals on them. The names of the ships were the *Cow,* the *Horse,* the *Sheep,* and the *Pig.* What do you think was on each ship?

Finding Freedom in the Colonies

Massachusetts

The people had sailed on the *Mayflower* for more than sixty days. They were glad to be on land at last. "We must find a place to build a town soon," one man said. "Then our wives and children can leave the ship and come to land too."

Finding a place for the town was not easy. The Separatists wanted to build a town in Virginia. But a storm blew their ship off its course. Now they were far north of that place. They had to start a new colony. Do you think they worried? No, they trusted in God to help them.

The men found a place near the water. The place had once been an Indian town. There was room for houses and for fields. The Separatists worked hard to build a town. They called their colony *Plymouth*. Later it became part of a bigger colony called *Massachusetts*.

Maryland

The people in England could not worship God in their own way. They had to go to the king's church or leave the country. The Separatists left England first. Then the Puritans left. Soon another group wanted to leave. They were called *Catholics*.

George Calvert was a Catholic. He asked the king of England to give him land in America. George wanted to start a colony where his Catholic friends could worship freely. He would pay for all the things the settlers needed.

Clothes for a Maryland Settler

Suits	
Shirts	
Socks	
Shoes	

George and his son planned the colony well. They even told the settlers what to bring with them when they came. "Each man will need three suits, three shirts, three pairs of socks, and six pairs of shoes. Each family must bring a rug, two sets of sheets for a bed, and material to make a mattress." Why do you think so many pairs of shoes were required? Can you think of other things you would want to bring if you were a colonist?

Out from Massachusetts

New Hampshire and Connecticut

Do you remember what colony the Separatists began?
They started settlements that became part of the Massachusetts
Colony. More and more people came to that colony. Soon
the people began to feel crowded. They moved away from
the big towns. They built new towns like Weymouth, Salem,
Sandwich, and Taunton.

Soon the new towns were crowded too. What do you think
some people did then? This time they moved even farther
away. They wanted more room to build farms and to hunt.
They wanted to trade with other groups of Indians. The new
towns they built became parts of new colonies. They called
these new colonies New Hampshire and Connecticut.

Rhode Island

Some people left the Massachusetts Colony for another reason. They did not agree with things other people said and did. Roger Williams was a preacher. He moved away from Massachusetts because he did not agree with the other preachers.

Roger lived with the Indians during the cold winter. When summer came, his family came to live with the Indians too. Roger paid the Indians for the land he lived on. Soon other people came to live in the tiny colony. Roger's colony was smaller than any other colony. But it had the longest name. Roger called it *The Colony of Rhode Island and Providence Plantations.*

Gifts from the King

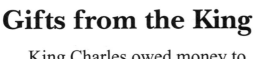

King Charles owed money to many people. Those people had helped him to become king. "How will I thank them?" he asked himself. "I do not have the money to pay them all. I will give them land in America instead."

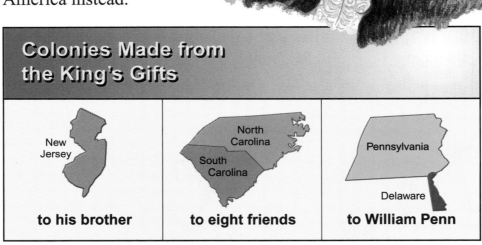

Colonies Made from the King's Gifts

New Jersey	North Carolina / South Carolina	Pennsylvania / Delaware
to his brother	**to eight friends**	**to William Penn**

New Jersey and the Carolinas

King Charles gave most of the land to his brother, James. Then James used the land to pay some men who had helped him too. He gave part of his land to two men. They called their new colony *New Jersey.* They named it for one of the men's homes, the island of Jersey.

The king gave some land to eight men. The men called their colony *Carolina*. Just like the men in Virginia, these men found a plant that made them rich. Their plant was *rice.* Do you like rice?

Rice was a hard plant to grow. The farmers needed more help. They bought people to help grow the rice. They called these people *slaves.* Do you think that the farmers did the right thing? The slaves' work made the rice farmers very rich. But the farmers did not share the money with their slaves. And they would not let them leave the farms. Would you have wanted to be a slave?

Later, the big Carolina Colony split into two colonies. The people there called one colony *North Carolina* and the other colony *South Carolina.* What do these names tell you about the new colonies?

William Penn's Colonies

William Penn was always in trouble. He was a part of a group of people called the Quakers. Other people in England did not like the Quakers. But two very important people liked him—the king and his brother, James.

King Charles told William, "I will give you land in America. You may go there with your Quakers."

Therefore all things whatsoever ye would that men should do to you, do ye even so to them.

Matthew 7:12

"I will call the land *Pennsylvania,*" said the king.

The name means "Penn's Woods." What does the name tell you about the land?

William Penn was glad to have a colony for the Quakers. But he wanted to let other people live in Pennsylvania too. And when some towns wanted to break away and become a new colony, Penn agreed. He called the new colony *Delaware.*

The Last Colony

James Oglethorpe visited a friend in prison. In England, people went to prison when they could not pay their bills. James was sad when he saw the dirt and sickness in the prison. He wanted to help the poor people that had to go there.

James went to the king. He asked him for land in America to start a new colony. Why do you think James wanted to make a colony? It would be for poor people who could not pay their bills. They could go to the colony instead of to prison.

King George II gave James some land in America. James named his colony *Georgia,* after King George. Can you find Georgia on a map?

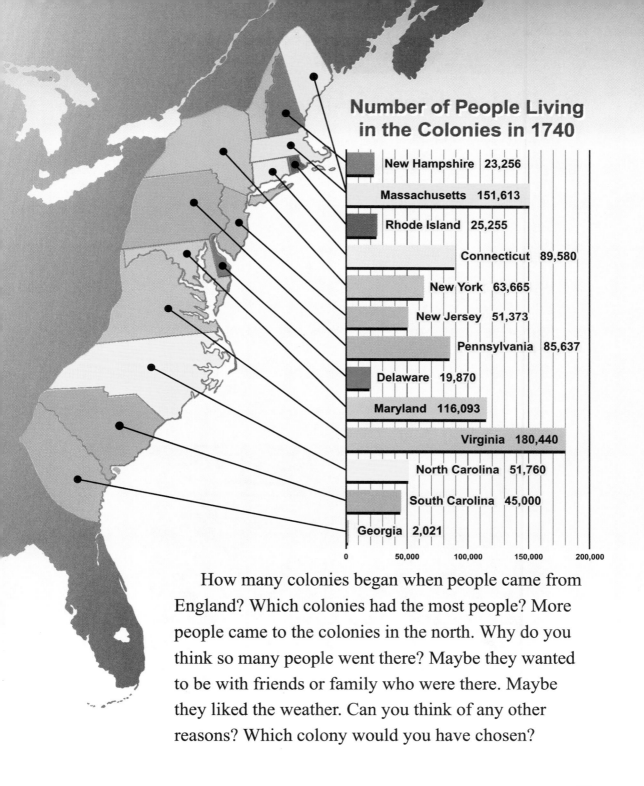

Number of People Living in the Colonies in 1740

New Hampshire	23,256
Massachusetts	151,613
Rhode Island	25,255
Connecticut	89,580
New York	63,665
New Jersey	51,373
Pennsylvania	85,637
Delaware	19,870
Maryland	116,093
Virginia	180,440
North Carolina	51,760
South Carolina	45,000
Georgia	2,021

How many colonies began when people came from England? Which colonies had the most people? More people came to the colonies in the north. Why do you think so many people went there? Maybe they wanted to be with friends or family who were there. Maybe they liked the weather. Can you think of any other reasons? Which colony would you have chosen?

To Read and Make a Bar Graph

1. Get your Notebook and some colored pencils or crayons.

2. Look at the picture graph on Notebook page 15. Picture graphs compare things. What does this picture graph compare? Bar graphs are like picture graphs. Your teacher will make this picture graph a bar graph. On the bar graph, each bar stands for the number of students in Miss McKee's class who chose each colony. Which colony was chosen by the fewest number of students?

3. Look at the empty bar graph at the bottom of the page. Use the pencils to color the graph as your teacher tells you.

4

People
from All Over

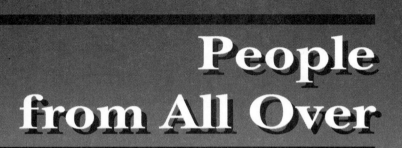

Where Did the Colonists Come From?

The colonies grew as more people came from Europe. You know some of the reasons that people came to live in the colonies. But do you know what countries the people left behind?

Look at the map. Can you tell which place the most people came from? Most of the people came from England. But people came from other places too. Can you name some of these other places?

People came from places like Ireland, Germany, France, Scotland, Sweden, and Africa. Someone from Germany was called a *German*. But when he came to the colonies, he was a *colonist*. Someone from Sweden was called a Swede. What was he called after he came to America?

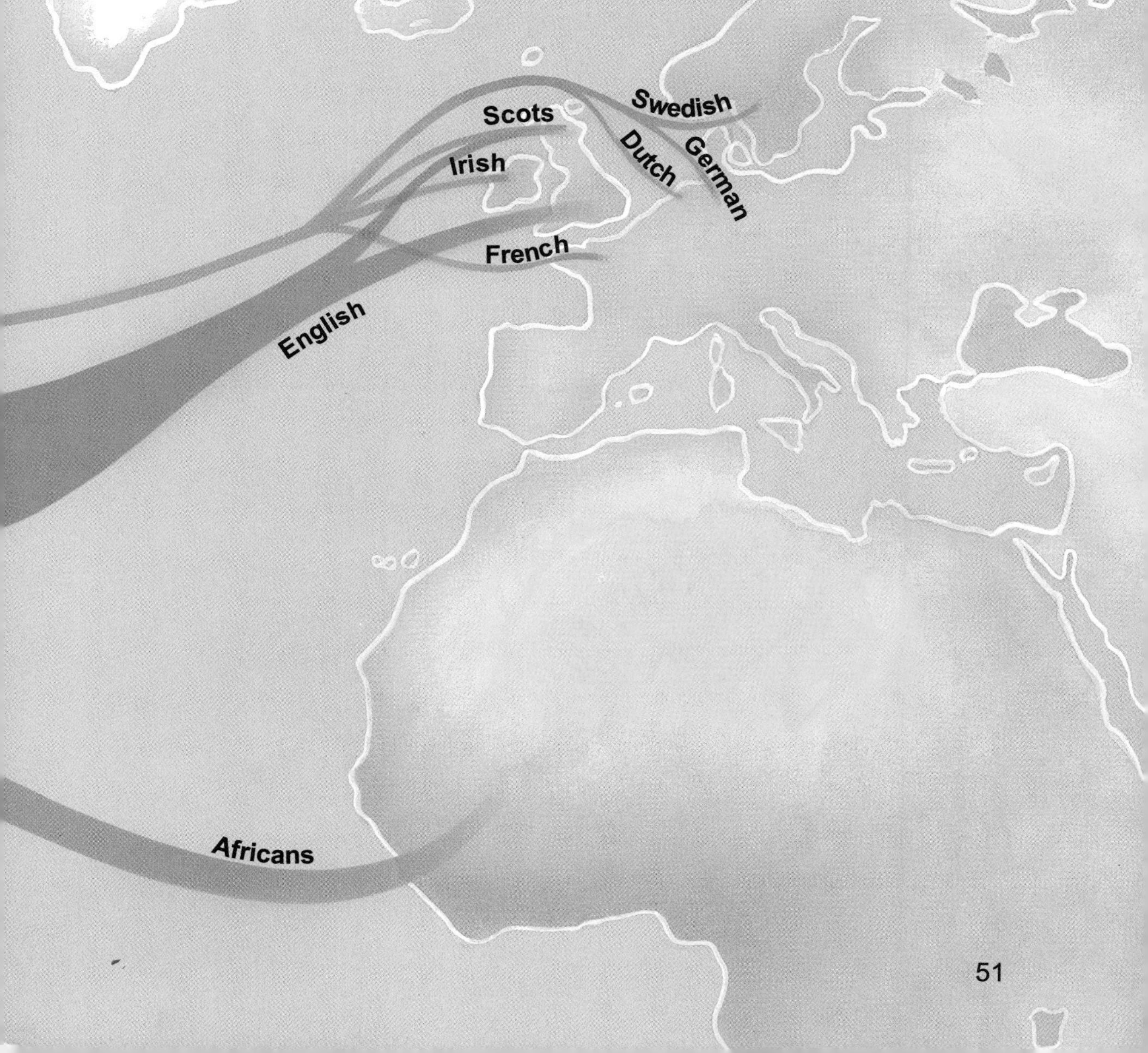

Scots

Irish

Swedish

Dutch

German

French

English

Africans

Homes in the Colonies

The people who came to live in the colonies did not find homes already built for them. They had to build their own homes from things they could find. Some of the very first colonists built places to live from branches, mud, and grass. Would you like to live in a home made from these things?

As soon as they could, the colonists made bigger, more sturdy houses. They remembered the homes they had left behind in their old countries. The new homes they built looked very much like those old homes. Which home looks most like your home?

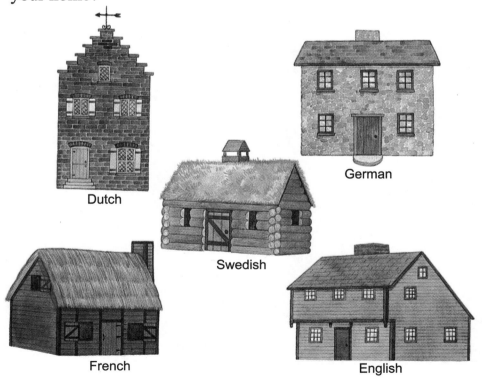

Dutch

German

Swedish

French

English

The Dutch colonists built houses like the one below. What do you think the houses they had left in their old country looked like? The houses were built of brick and wood. Some things would be found only in a Dutch home. Look at the brick part of this house. Would you like to climb the steps at the top of the wall? Boys sometimes did. The wall was built with steps to make it easy for boys to climb up to clean the chimney.

Most Dutch homes had a special door with two parts. The top part of the door could be opened to let in air. Ladies liked to stand at the door and talk to their friends. Keeping the bottom of the door closed kept the little children in and the pigs and ducks and sheep out.

Good Things to Eat

The colonists raised most of the food they ate. Even the colonists who lived in towns and cities grew their own food in gardens behind their houses. Many city families had chickens, cows, goats, and pigs too. What things to eat did they get from these animals?

Colonists got many seeds for their gardens from the Indians. The Indians gave them seeds for pumpkin, corn, squash, peppers, and beans. But colonists brought some seeds with them from their old country. From these seeds they grew some of their favorite foods—carrots, turnips, spinach, and fruits.

Do you have a favorite fruit? Many colonists liked apples. The colonists fixed apples many different ways. They ate them whole, made applesauce or pie, or pressed out the juice and made apple cider. Which way do you like to eat apples?

Look at this table. What things will you see when you sit down to eat today? You probably will not see plates like these. Most of the colonists used wooden plates called *trenchers*. Often, two people would share one trencher. The colonists used spoons and knives to eat their food. Will you use a spoon or knife? What else might you use to eat your food?

How many cups do you see on this table? Everyone in the family drank from the same cup. If guests came for dinner, they drank from that cup too. Only very rich colonists had more than one cup for drinking.

Phillis Wheatley
(1753-1784)

Phillis Wheatley was a slave. She came to the colonies when she was just seven years old. A man named John Wheatley bought her. He hoped that she would be a good helper for his wife.

Most slaves did not know how to read or write. Even many white ladies did not know how to do these things. But Mr. Wheatley and his wife knew that Phillis was smart. They taught Phillis how to read and write.

Phillis liked to read. And poems were her favorite thing to read. Soon she tried writing poems. When she was only nineteen years old, some of her poems were put in a book. Her poems told about God's love. They told about things that happened in the colonies. Sometimes they told about special people. Phillis was America's first black poet.

Pretty Things

The colonists loved pretty things. When they could, they brought pretty things with them to their new country. But many times these things were too big or too heavy to bring. The tiny ships could not carry much.

Some French ladies found a way to bring something pretty. They put flower seeds in their apron pockets. What do you think they did with the seeds? They kept them until they built a new home. Then they planted the seeds. Hollyhocks and primroses made their small homes cheery.

Soon the colonists could make or buy pretty things. Some people wanted to decorate their new homes. They made colorful quilts. They bought silver cups. A few people even wanted pictures of themselves. They hung the pictures on the wall. Pictures like this one are called *limnings*.

To Make a Limning

1. Get a pencil, some crayons, and the paper your teacher will give you.

2. Take out the Notebook page your teacher tells you to. Listen as your teacher tells you about limnings. Then choose someone to draw. Draw his or her face in the right place on the page.

3. Color the picture if you like. Can the person you drew recognize himself? Why do you think artists painted limnings?

Everyday and Special Days

The colonists knew how to turn everyday work into fun. If a colonist had a big job to do, he asked other people to help. They might work together to take stumps and stones from a field. They might build a house or a barn. They might even make maple syrup out of maple tree sap.

Then when they had finished the job, the colonists would have a party. The ladies would bring pies and cakes and other good things to eat. The men would carry in a big barrel full of apple cider. What good things to eat can you see? Would you help with the work so that you could come to this party?

Holding a Fair

Have you ever been to a county fair? People have held fairs for many hundreds of years. Some colonists had seen such fairs in their old countries. They brought the idea of holding fairs to the colonies.

The colonists' fairs were very much like our fairs today. The Dutch colonists celebrated a holiday called *kermis* with a fair. Sometimes this fair lasted six weeks. People came from other towns and colonies. They came to show things they had made. They came to buy things from others too.

Each day the fair opened at noon. Some colonists spent the day looking at the cows, pigs, and other animals. Others tasted the good cheeses and cakes for sale. Children could always be found watching the puppet shows or the dancing bear or looking at the toys for sale. What thing would you like to see or do?

Election Day was a special day for the English colonists. What do you think the people did on Election Day? They elected, or voted for, their leaders. The person with the most votes became the colonists' leader. Sometimes the fun of Election Day went on for almost a week.

Sunday was a special day for all the colonists. No one worked hard on Sunday. In some colonies there were laws that said things like "Do not work on Sunday. Do not play on Sunday. Do not run or laugh on Sunday." Do you know what the colonists did that day? They went to church to pray and to listen to preaching.

All the churches were not the same. Dutch churches were different from French churches. English churches were different from German churches. African churches were different from other churches too. Some slaves went to church where their masters did. But other slaves had their own churches. The preachers taught them Bible stories. The people liked to hear about heaven.

The African people had their own songs too. They liked to sing about how God rescues people from bad times. Why do you think so many of their songs were about freedom? As slavery increased, African churches grew and more songs about freedom gave hope to the people.

The Lord is my strength and song, and is become my salvation.
Psalm 118:14

Enfield, Connecticut
July 8, 1741

Many years after the Separatists came to the colonies, most people still went to church each Sunday. They still did good works. But they did not know God.

These people had come to hear Jonathan Edwards preach. He told them that they were sinners.

Pastor Edwards preached from God's Word. He told the people how God feels about their sin.

The people knew that Pastor Edwards was right. As he spoke, the people began to kneel. They prayed out loud. They were sorry for their sins, and they asked God to forgive them. Later they would tell others what they had heard.

The colonies were made up of many different kinds of people. The people spoke different languages. They ate different kinds of foods. They had fun in different ways. They even had different ways of worshiping God. Together, the different people living in each colony made it the kind of place it was.

Today our country is made up of different kinds of people, just as it was back then. The differences make our country a special place to live. People still come from other countries. When they make a new home here, they are still called by a new name. They are called *Americans*.

5

Communities Grow

Growing and Changing

Look at these pictures.
Which one do you think was taken first?

Why do you think so? What things are different in the second picture?

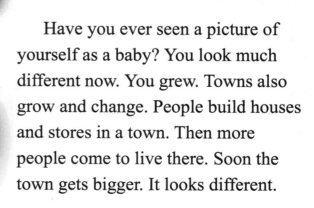

Have you ever seen a picture of yourself as a baby? You look much different now. You grew. Towns also grow and change. People build houses and stores in a town. Then more people come to live there. Soon the town gets bigger. It looks different.

Places can become towns in different ways. Sometimes a group of people build houses close together. Plymouth Plantation began as a row of eight houses and a fort and a governor's house. In five years the town grew to twenty-two houses. Two even rows of houses faced each other. How many houses were in each row?

Other towns did not begin in neat rows. Look at the picture map. Where did the people of this town build most of their houses? Why do you think they are not in rows?

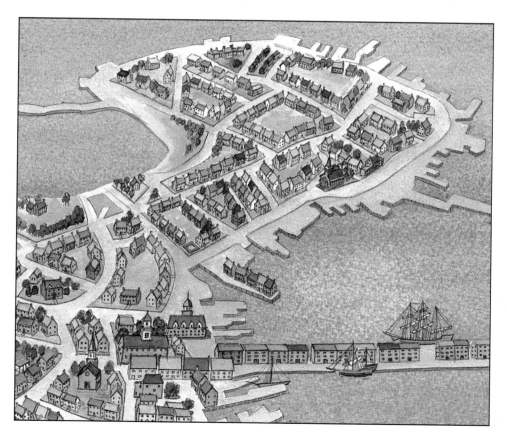

How Towns Grow

A few places were carefully planned. A man named William Penn wanted a map for the city of Philadelphia. He wanted the people to build their houses and stores by his plan.

William Penn had a man draw a picture of how Philadelphia should look. Here is a copy of William Penn's plan. What do you think of it? Where would you have built a house?

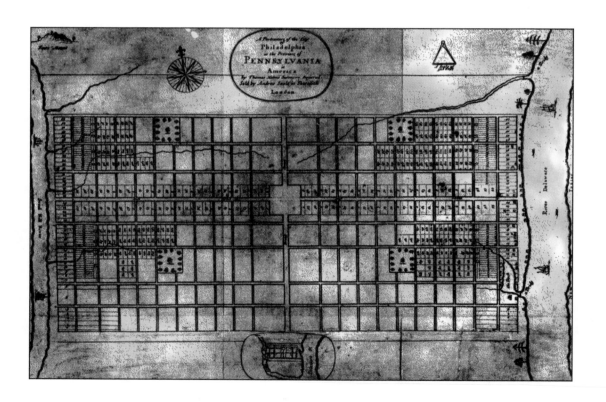

Your Town Grew

1. Take home the Fact Finder your teacher gives you. Show it to your parents or your neighbors. Ask them to help you fill in the answers to the questions.

2. Make a booklet about your town. Use the Fact Finder and pictures your parents and neighbors have given you.

Maps stand for real places. When real towns and cities grow, maps have to be changed. Look at the two maps on these pages.

What buildings have been added since the first map? Have any new streets been made? What other changes do you see?

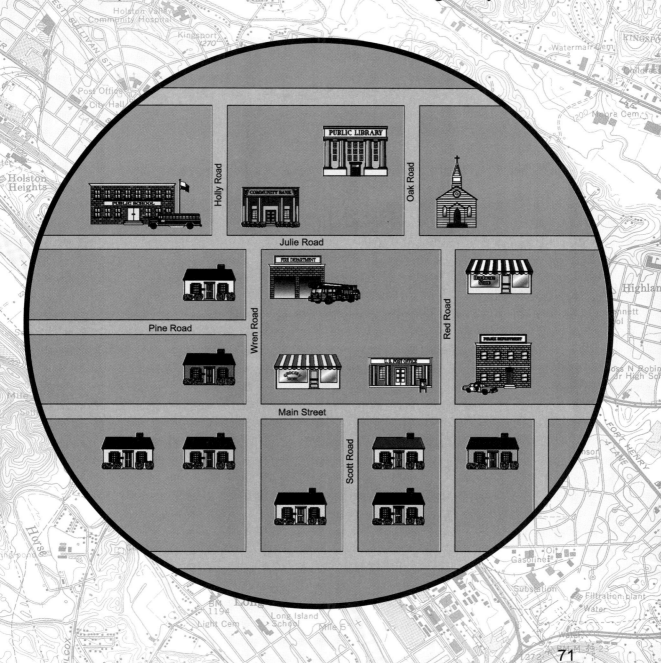

Counting How Many Live in a Town

Have you ever gone to a new city or town? Did you see a sign that said "Population" and then a number? *Population* means "how many people live in a place." How many people live in your town?

How do you think the leaders of towns count people? Would you like to try to count all the people in New York City? All cities, towns, and villages in the United States count people every ten years.

The counting is called a *census.* The leaders send out a paper to every house. The people write down how many people live in the house. Special workers add up all the numbers on all the papers. The census is not perfect; it can tell us only about how many people live in our country.

Maps Matter

Bigger maps show how many cities and towns are in a country. This map shows the cities and towns in our country about 300 years ago. Can you find Philadelphia? Is it north or south of Boston? Can you find Plymouth? Who started the town of Plymouth? The Pilgrims and the Separatists did.

One of the girls from the *Mayflower* got married. She left Plymouth with her husband. They went to Boston. Which way did they go? Can you trace with your finger the path people might have taken from Boston to Philadelphia?

Boston •
Plymouth •

Philadelphia •

Why do we need good maps? Maps help us get from place to place. They help us record how places look.

People tell each other how to get from one place to another. They give *directions.* Can you give directions from your home to your church? Ask someone to give you directions to his home. Do you think you could follow them?

And Jesus went about all the cities and villages, teaching in their synagogues, and preaching the gospel of the kingdom.

Matthew 9:35

Pieter Jan Van Reysschoot, Christ Teaching on the Mountain, *The Bob Jones University Collection*

6

Shopkeeping

The Print Shop

"Ben," said James, "bring me that stack of paper." Ben ran to get the paper. And then he ran back to the room he had come from. He was helping to put small blocks of wood with letters on them on a big board.

Then he picked up a stuffed leather pouch by its stick handle. He pushed the pouch into some ink. Then he squashed the inky pouch over the blocks with the letters on them. What do you think the boy was doing?

Ben was helping to print a newspaper. After the letters had ink on them, a man put a huge sheet of paper over them. Then he laid a piece of flat wood over that. He turned a big handle and made the wood press down on the paper. What do you think happened to the paper? The letter blocks printed words on the paper. Why is a printing press called a press?

"Ben," said the printer, "take these newspapers. Go out in the street and sell them." Ben left the shop and took a bundle of papers outside.

"Buy a paper!" Ben called. "Buy a paper!" People came up to him. They gave him money. He gave them papers. Why do you think a boy so young worked so hard all day?

Ben was learning to be a printer. He was an *apprentice*. An apprentice helped with work to learn to do it himself. Ben worked for his brother. He was supposed to work there until he was twenty-one. It might take ten years to learn to be a printer.

Benjamin Franklin
(1706-1790)

Ben Franklin did become a printer. He made books. But he also did many other things. He invented a new stove and a kind of eyeglasses. He made a rocking chair. And he proved that lightning and electricity are the same.

When Ben was a boy, he invented things for fun. Once he made paddles for his hands; he thought they would help him swim faster. Do you think the paddles worked? They helped him swim faster, but they hurt his hands.

Ben Franklin became an important American. He knew about a lot of things. He could speak well. He made friends easily. When the American colonies became the United States, Ben Franklin was ready to help.

The Blacksmith's Shop

Clank! Clank! The sparks flew from under the iron hammer. A big man in a leather apron called out, "Peter, more heat." The boy pulled down on a handle, and air blew into the fire. The fire got hotter.

The big man, a *blacksmith,* turned to the fire. He stuck an iron rod in the flames. The end got so hot that it was red. When it turned orange, he pulled it out. Then he banged it again with the hammer.

The blacksmith made nails and hinges and horseshoes and many other things that the colonists needed. Sometimes he put shoes on horses. Would you like to see someone shoe a horse?

Peter was the blacksmith's apprentice. One of his jobs was to work the *bellows*. The bellows worked something like an accordian works. But they did not make music. They blew air into the fire to make it burn better.

A man came into the shop. He had built a new house. He wanted a weathervane. The blacksmith took the job. Peter was happy. He liked to watch the blacksmith make fancy pieces.

Do you think a blacksmith had to be strong? He had to lift heavy pieces of metal many times a day. He also had to be alert. He had to know and understand the colors that metals turn in the fire.

Peter became a blackmith. He ran his own shop. He was one of the best blacksmiths anywhere. He had apprentices who worked for him. He was kind to his workers. Why do you think he was kind?

The most important job Peter ever did was to make a huge chain. Each link in the chain was three feet long—as long as a yardstick. The chain was as long as five football fields. What do you think the chain was for?

It kept enemy ships out of the Hudson River. The chain held. What if Peter had not done his work well?

Masters, give unto your servants that which is just and equal; knowing that ye also have a Master in heaven.

Colossians 4:1

Making Up Sayings

What does someone mean when he says you should use "lowercase letters"? He means you should not use capital letters. Capital letters are called "uppercase" letters. Printers used to keep the blocks of wood with capital letters on them in a top drawer or an "upper case." What do you think they kept in the bottom drawer?

When the time is right to do something, people say, "Strike while the iron is hot." What shop do you think that phrase came from? It came from the blacksmith's shop. The blacksmith knew he had to hit the metal when it was still red from the fire. Now the phrase means you must do something quickly, before time runs out.

The Shoemaker's Shop

The Plymouth settlers brought extra shoes with them. But shoes wear out. They needed someone to make more shoes. How else might they get shoes? They could send back to England for some. Some people wore Indian shoes called *moccasins*.

A man decided to take his shoemaking shop to America. He told his apprentice, "I'll be the only shoemaker. I'll make a lot of money, Richard." He began to pack his tools.

Richard did not want to leave England. He was afraid of the long boat trip on the ocean. He did not want to leave his friends. Do you think he went?

Richard had to go with the shoemaker. An apprentice signed a paper when he went to work for someone. The paper said that the apprentice would work for seven years or longer. It also said that he had to do whatever the master said.

Richard did as he had promised. He obeyed his master and went to America. When his time was up, he went back to England. Why do you think he did not stay? Why is it important to do what you say you will?

Shoes were made of leather. Sometimes the heels were made of wood. What are your shoes made of? Do you know where leather comes from? Leather is made from animal skins.

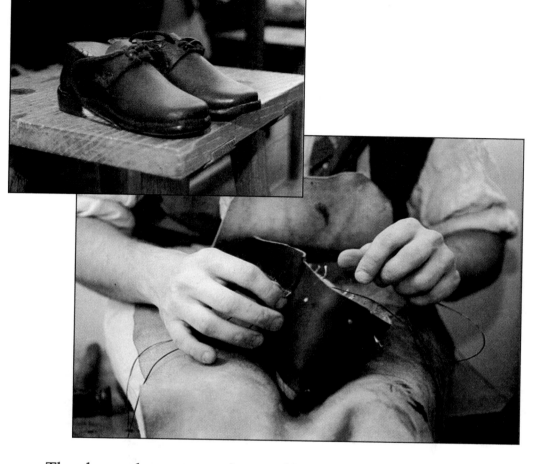

The shoemaker cut out pieces of leather to make the top of the shoe and sewed them together. Then he put the bottom of the shoe on a metal frame and beat the leather with a hammer. The beating helped the shoe last longer when it was worn.

The shoemaker then glued and sewed the top and bottom of the shoe together. If the shoes were for special times, he might color the heels red. Usually the shoes were colored all dark brown or black.

To Make a Shoe

1. Get your Notebook, some scissors, some cloth, some glue, and two pieces of cardboard.

2. Cut out the patterns. Cut a sole and an insole from the cardboard, using the patterns. Cut out the other pieces of the shoe from the cloth.

3. Put the shoe together. Your teacher will show you how. Do you think your shoe will fit? Do you think it will wear well?

Learning a Trade

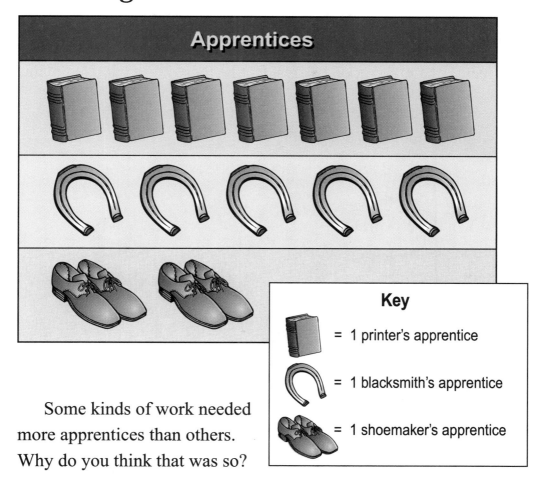

Apprentices

Key

= 1 printer's apprentice

= 1 blacksmith's apprentice

= 1 shoemaker's apprentice

Some kinds of work needed more apprentices than others. Why do you think that was so?

This graph shows how many apprentices worked in a town. How many blacksmith's apprentices were there? How many printer's apprentices? How many shoemaker's apprentices?

Do you think this town had few people in it or many? What makes you say so?

The Cooper's Shop
June 15, 1774

Neptune Thurston worked for a cooper, or barrel maker. He learned to make good barrels. But he thought they looked plain.

So he drew pictures on them. Sometimes he drew pictures of the people who bought the barrels.

A boy in the shop watched him draw on the barrels. When the boy grew up, he became a famous painter. He said, "I learned to draw by watching Neptune Thurston."

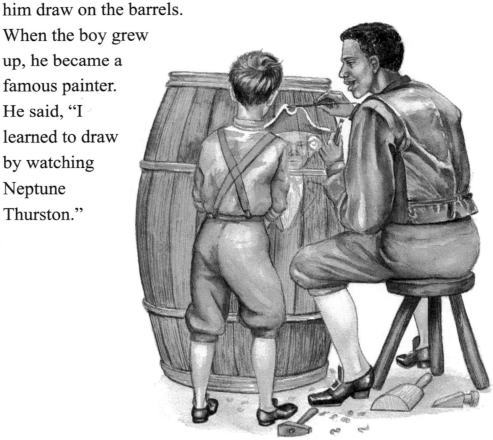

Printers, blacksmiths, and shoemakers all worked at their trades for a living. Sometimes people paid them with money. Sometimes people did work to get a book or a tool. Sometimes people exchanged one thing for another.

Suppose a blacksmith wanted a new pair of shoes for his son. And suppose the shoemaker needed another metal piece to hammer leather on. What do you think the two workers might do? Each might make the thing the other needed and then make an exchange.

What did apprentices exchange for learning a job? They exchanged their work. What work did Ben do at the print shop? What did Richard and Peter do at their shops? Would you like to be an apprentice? What would you learn to do?

Today many people go to schools to learn trades. Then they get a job and learn more about the work they have chosen. Some places still have apprentices.

There are schools that teach modern trades. Some teach students how to fix cars. Some teach farming. Some teach how to cut people's hair. Do you think people can still learn to be printers, blacksmiths, and shoemakers? Yes, they can.

Long ago apprentices did not often get to choose what work they learned to do. Their fathers chose for them. Most fathers tried to find what their children would like. Today many people choose their work themselves. What work do you think about doing someday?

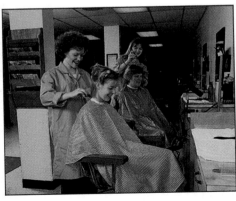

7

Kings and
Queens

Who Rules These Kingdoms?

In the American colonies, a blacksmith hammered at his anvil. Some farmers scythed the hay in the fields. Ben Franklin worked to make a better stove. King George ruled from far away in England. But the colonists were not the only people in the world. And King George was not the only ruler.

Look at the map above. It shows countries where kings or queens ruled when King George did. Each color stands for a different king. How many kingdoms do you see?

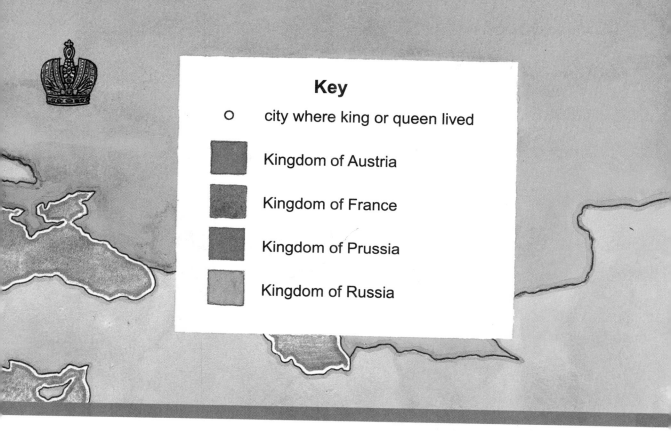

Key

○   city where king or queen lived

   Kingdom of Austria

   Kingdom of France

   Kingdom of Prussia

   Kingdom of Russia

Some rulers were kind and giving. They loved and served the people in their kingdoms. Other rulers were not kind. They took money from the poor people of their kingdoms. Then they spent the money. They bought fancy clothes and beautiful places to live. Sometimes they spent money on parties and gifts for their rich friends too. Which kind of king would you like better?

As a roaring lion, and a ranging bear; so is a wicked ruler over the poor people.
                             Proverbs 28:15

King Louis

Little Prince Louis became king of France when he was just five years old. Many kings in that country had been called Louis. His great-grandfather was Louis the Fourteenth. What number do you think followed Little Louis's name? He was Louis the Fifteenth.

Before Little Louis became king, his great-grandfather told him how to be a good king. Great-grandfather Louis said, "Do not fight with other kings. I have fought too many wars. Do not spend money on wars or on fancy things for yourself."

Do you know any five-year-olds who could rule a whole country? King Louis was not ready to rule. Louis's helpers ruled for him. The helpers remembered the things that Louis's great-grandfather told him.
They did not fight with other kings.
They did not build new palaces
or hold fancy parties.

When King Louis grew up, he wanted to rule his country by himself. Do you think he remembered his great-grandfather's words? He made his people fight a war with the people from England. He lost the war. And he lost all his land in America.

Even losing the war did not make King Louis remember his great-grandfather's words. He gave big parties for his rich friends. He bought new furniture for his palace. Would you like to live in a home like this?

Making Furniture

Years ago people made furniture by hand. Do you know what furniture is? Tables, chairs, and beds are *furniture*. Men used special tools to make the tables and beds. They used other tools to carve flowers and animals in the wood.

King Louis asked some men to make furniture for his palace. He wanted it to be different from any other kind of furniture. We call this kind of furniture *Louis XV* furniture.

Today most furniture is made in factories. Many people use machines to work on each table or bed. But some people still make beautiful furniture by hand. Have you ever seen any handmade furniture?

Frederick the Great

Prince Frederick knew that one day he would be king of the country his father ruled. But he did not want to be king of Prussia. He wanted to play his flute and to write music and poetry. When Frederick was a young man, he left his father's palace. Maybe he thought the king would choose someone else to rule next. What do you think his father did?

The king loved his son. He wanted Prince Frederick to be a good ruler. The king sent men after Frederick, and they brought him back home.

Prince Frederick made up his mind to work hard to please his father. He learned to lead the army. He learned to make wise choices. Then his father told him, "Prince Frederick, you may write poetry and play your flute when you finish your other work."

The time soon came for Frederick to be king. He knew he had learned his lessons well. His armies won many fights. He added new lands to his kingdom. Why do you think King Frederick wanted these new lands? These lands had coal and iron mines. The mines helped to make Prussia a rich country.

Queen Maria Theresa

The royal palace in the city of Vienna hummed. Everyone there was very excited. A beautiful baby girl had just been born. Her father said, "We will call her Maria Theresa Walburga Amalia Christina." Would you like to have a name that long? Some people may have thought it was too long a name for such a tiny baby. But it was a perfect name for a princess.

King Charles tried to be excited too. It was not easy. He was very happy to have a healthy daughter. But he had hoped for a son. Why do you think the king wanted a son?

King Charles ruled many countries. He prayed for a son who could rule those countries one day. But a son was not born in the royal palace. The time came for King Charles to choose someone new to rule his countries. He would need to teach the new ruler to be a wise leader. Whom do you think he chose?

Princess Maria Theresa was kind, honest, and smart. King Charles knew that she would make a good queen. Although his countries had always been ruled by a king, King Charles chose Maria Theresa to be the next ruler.

Kings who ruled in other places said, "We want Princess Maria Theresa to rule her father's kingdom. We think Maria Theresa will make a good ruler too. We promise we will not send our armies to attack her."

Do you think the other kings kept their promises to King Charles? They did not. They began to fight with the kingdom soon after King Charles died. Maria Theresa put on the royal robes and crown. She carried the royal shield. She climbed onto a black stallion and rode to the top of the Royal Mount. She showed that she was ready to fight for her kingdom. The people cheered.

The people called Queen Maria Theresa their "mother." How do you think they felt about their queen? They fought hard and helped her to keep most of her kingdom.

Carrying a Coat of Arms

Long ago every man carried a shield to defend himself in a fight. Each shield showed one or more pictures. The pictures stood for the good deeds and traits of the person who carried it. The men called the pictures a *coat of arms.*

Before long sons and grandsons began to use the coat of arms of one of their important ancestors. The coat of arms became a family symbol. People in the family remembered to do the good deeds of their ancestor each time they saw the pictures.

Today most families do not use a coat of arms. But some shields with pictures like a coat of arms are well known to every American.

Have you ever seen shields that look like these? What do you think the pictures stand for?

103

Catherine the Great

Sophia Augusta Frederica was the daughter of a prince and a princess. What do you think her life was like? Sophia did not grow up in a lovely palace. She did not have servants and rich playmates. Her parents were not rich; she spent most of her childhood alone in a cold, drab castle.

When Princess Sophia was just fourteen years old, her quiet life changed forever. Her parents told her, "You must marry the prince of Russia." For the next two years, Sophia studied hard. She learned about the people of Russia. She learned to speak the way they did. And she learned to do things the Russian way. She even gave herself a new name: Catherine.

Even though Catherine did not love Prince Peter, she decided to marry him. She wanted to be a queen of a large country. But she knew that Prince Peter would not make a good king. Why do you think she married someone who would not make a good king?

Catherine tried hard to make the people in Russia like her. It worked—most people liked Catherine more than they liked Prince Peter! Catherine finally became a queen when Prince Peter became King Peter. Do you think that made her happy? It did not. Only six months later, she was ruling Russia by herself.

Queen Catherine liked to read and to write. She wrote letters to famous people in other countries. She told them that she believed that all people are equal. She said she wanted to help the poor people of Russia. The rich people treated them like slaves. Catherine always meant to help them. But she never could decide how to do it.

To Write a Letter

1. Get a pencil and a clean piece of paper. Your teacher will give you the name of a person to write at the top of the piece of paper.

2. Think about yourself. How many people are in your family? What things do you like to do? Write about these things.

3. Think about the person you are writing to. Do you know him? What things would you like to know about him? Write these things on the paper too.

4. Sign your name at the bottom of the paper in the place your teacher shows you. What else must you do before the letter can be sent?

Some kings and queens ruled their countries wisely. Some did not. Who allowed all kings and queens to rule? God let them rule. Do you think God watches over other leaders too?

By me kings reign,
and princes decree justice.
By me princes rule,
and nobles, even all the
judges of the earth.
Proverbs 8:15-16

Master of Riofrio, David the Prophet
The Bob Jones University Collection

8

Kings
Make Rules

By Order of the King

If you were king of a country, what kind of rules would you make? Would you make rules that would help you? Or would you make rules that would help the people of the country? Would you remember that God puts kings on thrones and that God can take them off those thrones?

Real kings made both kinds of rules, or *laws,* for their people. Many times kings did and said anything they wanted. No one could tell them what to do. If the king was kind, he would try to make good laws. If he was not, he did not care whether the law was good or bad. He cared only that he got what he wanted. Do you think he was humble before God?

King Louis XIV of France made laws that helped him get rich. But no matter how much he had, Louis was never happy.

Louis XIV sent soldiers to the New World. He told them, "Keep all the land you can and get more. I want more land." The soldiers sailed away. Do you think he sent a few soldiers or many? He sent many.

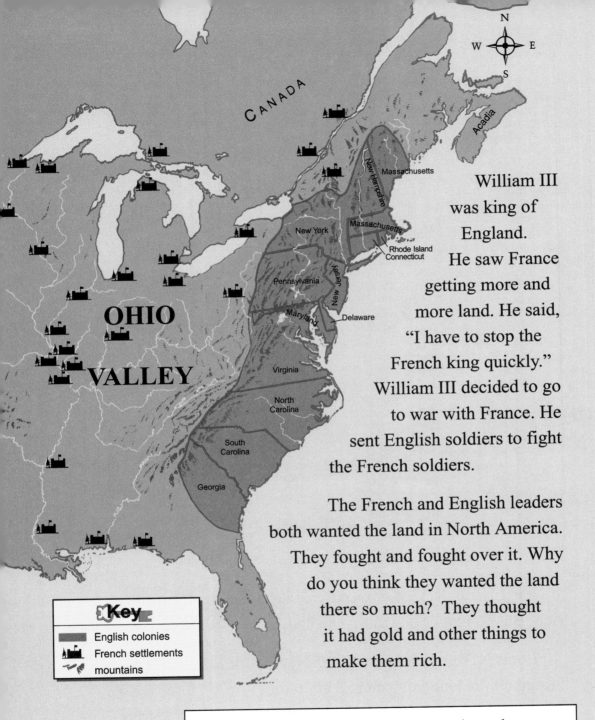

CANADA

Acadia

N
W E
S

New Hampshire

Massachusetts

New York

Massachusetts

Rhode Island
Connecticut

OHIO

Pennsylvania

New Jersey

Delaware

Maryland

VALLEY

Virginia

North
Carolina

South
Carolina

Georgia

Key

English colonies
French settlements
mountains

William III was king of England. He saw France getting more and more land. He said, "I have to stop the French king quickly." William III decided to go to war with France. He sent English soldiers to fight the French soldiers.

The French and English leaders both wanted the land in North America. They fought and fought over it. Why do you think they wanted the land there so much? They thought it had gold and other things to make them rich.

Look at the map. Did the French settle east or west of the mountains? Did the English or the French live in Canada? Can you find Acadia?

On the Same Side—
The French and the Indians

The French soldiers made friends with some of the Indian tribes. They said, "We will give you guns and gifts if you will help us fight." Many Indians sided with the French.

The French soldiers and some Indians attacked an English town. They killed people and animals and took many goods. Many of the Indians helped the French. Some people later began to call the fighting *the French and Indian Wars.*

How do you think the English King William felt? He was angry. He wanted to get back at the French. His men tried to get Indians on his side. Some Indians went to help the English.

Door from the house above, still showing the marks made by tomahawks during the French and Indian Wars

To Sing a French Song

1. Listen to the song your teacher sings or plays for you.

2. Practice saying the words with your teacher.

3. Sing the words to the tune. Now you are singing a song the French soldiers might have sung.

Fighting the French and Indian Wars

Both English and French soldiers had to be paid. And the soldiers needed more bullets and guns and food. Where do you think the kings got money to pay the soldiers? Do you think they used their own money? No, they did not. They made the people of their countries give the money.

Kings can get money from their people with *taxes*. Have you ever heard someone talking about paying his taxes? What do you think he meant? If a leader says everyone must pay some money to help the country, he is making a *tax*. Do you think people like to pay taxes? They usually do not.

The French people had to pay taxes. The English people had to pay taxes. The American people had to pay taxes too. None of the people had a choice. The kings did not let them vote on the taxes. The people just had to pay the money.

The French taxes paid the soldiers fighting for France. The English and American money paid the soldiers fighting for England. Pretend you are a farmer in America. You have just enough money to feed your family. Would you like to pay taxes to the king?

Queen Anne became leader of England. What do you think she did about the French soldiers and the Indians in the New World? She sent part of her army to fight them. She did not want the French to have North America either.

After Queen Anne, King George I, and King George II came King George III. Do you think he wanted the land too? Yes, he did. He kept fighting the French just as William and Anne had. Just as the kings and queen before him, George III fought the French.

Louis XV grew up in a great palace in France. But Louis XV did not learn how to make rules that helped his people. When he became king, he sent soldiers to the New World. Whose army did they fight?

The Biggest Battle

One of the biggest battles of the French and Indian Wars started along a muddy road in the middle of a forest. The English soldiers marched in the road. They were dressed in red coats with shiny buttons. Some American soldiers were there. They all were on their way to attack a French fort.

Some men had to go first and make a road. There was only a small path to begin with. They cut down trees and brush. Why did they have to make the road wide? There were many soldiers coming behind them.

Suddenly French soldiers and Indians shot at the English and the Americans from the forest. The lines of soldiers in red coats had nowhere to go. They had learned to fight in the open. Their leader told them to stay in the road. He said, "Fight as you were taught!"

Many English soldiers were killed. Even their leader was killed. One brave American got five bullet holes in his coat, but he was not hurt. His name was George Washington. He did not forget what he saw in that battle. He later became a leader in the American army.

Near a French Fort
July 9, 1755

Morning

French and Indians shot at English and American soldiers.
Many English and American soldiers were hurt.

George Washington said, "Let the English fight like Indians!"
The English leader said, "No! We will fight like Englishmen!"
The English leader was shot, and the English lost the battle.

The French and the English fought over the land in North America for many years. Sometimes the English won. Sometimes the French won. The French won the big battle that Daniel Boone and George Washington were in.

> *Or what king, going to make war against another king, sitteth not down first, and consulteth whether he be able with ten thousand to meet him that cometh against him with twenty thousand?*
>
> Luke 14:31

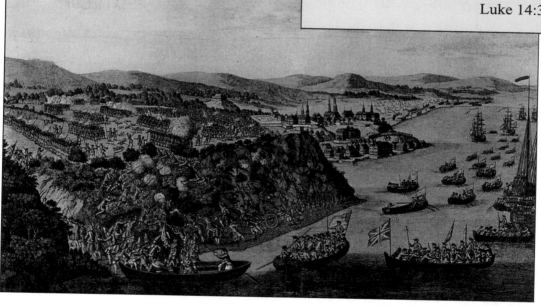

The English won the war at last. The French no longer could decide what would happen to America. For a while the Americans liked the English and King George III because the English had helped them fight off the French and the Indians. But that feeling was not to last long.

Daniel Boone
(1734-1820)

Daniel Boone was a Quaker and a hunter and a man of adventure. He liked to shoot bears and sleep outside. Once when he was a boy, he went out to get the cows. He came back two days later with bear meat and a bearskin for his mother.

When he was twenty years old, Boone saw a poster put out by Benjamin Franklin. The poster said anyone who drove a wagon for the English army would get good pay. Boone signed up. He was there at the big battle in the wilderness. He may have seen George Washington who fought in that battle.

After the battle, Boone went home, but not for long. He spent his whole life exploring. He went as far west as Yellowstone Lake and as far south as St. Augustine, Florida. He made Indian friends on his trips. An Indian chief adopted him and named him "Big Turtle."

Daniel Boone's home near Philadelphia

9

This Means War!

The Stamp Tax

The year was 1763. The war with the French and the Indians was finally over. The colonists had fought hard. They had given their lives and their money to help win the war. Now they thought things would get back to normal. What do you think?

King George had other ideas. The war had cost him a lot of money. He did not think the colonists had given their fair share. After all, had not the war been fought to help protect the colonies? Now they were safe from French attacks on their tiny settlements.

What would you have done if you were King George? He knew he must get money to pay for the war. He decided to make the colonists pay taxes. One of the first taxes he wanted them to pay was the stamp tax.

King George thought the stamp tax was a fair tax.
Everyone would have to pay it, both rich and poor.
The colonists would pay more for all kinds of printed
things—newspapers, contracts, school papers, and calendars.

The king's men did not gather the tax by selling stamps
like we use today. Instead, the men stamped a special design
into pieces of paper. Printers had to use these pieces of paper
when they printed newspapers or calendars.

Do you think this tax was a fair tax? The colonists did not think so. They would pay taxes made by their own leaders. But the colonists did not think they should pay taxes to the king in England. No king had ever asked them to pay taxes before. Besides, they did not want to pay taxes colonists had not voted for. And King George would not let the colonists vote.

The colonists decided they would not pay the tax. The lawyers closed their law offices. Printers quit printing papers. Some lawyers and printers still worked just as they always had. They just used the old, unstamped paper. Some men were very angry about the tax. They beat the men who were selling the stamped paper for the king. Do you think that was the right thing to do?

To Pay a Tax

1. Get a pencil, a pair of scissors, the paper coins from your teacher, an ink pad, a rubber stamp, and your schoolwork papers for the day.

2. Cut out the "money."

3. Your teacher will choose someone to be the tax collector. The tax collector will use the ink pad and rubber stamp.

4. Before turning in each page of schoolwork, pay the tax collector one piece of construction-paper money. He will use the rubber stamp to mark your paper "taxed." What will happen if you forget to pay the tax? How will you pay your stamp tax when you run out of money?

A New Tax Law

Soon King George saw that the Stamp Act was not working. He did not understand why the tax upset the colonists. Even so, he passed a law to end the stamp tax.

But King George still wanted to tax the colonists. What other things do you think he could tax? About one year later he made a new tax law. This law put a tax on all sorts of things brought from England. Now colonists could not buy things like tea, paint, window glass, paper, cloth, and lead unless they paid a tax. What do you think the colonists did?

The colonists said, "We do not need the things the king wants to tax." Their homes did not need paint so often. They did not need glass windows. And as much as they liked tea, they knew they could live without it. But there was one thing on the list they could not do without. What do you think it was?

Cloth was a thing the colonists could not do without. Holes appeared in the knees and elbows of favorite suits. Little boys and girls grew too big for their play clothes. Soon ladies in all the colonies learned to make their own cloth. Then they made new clothes for their families.

She seeketh wool, and flax, and worketh willingly with her hands. She layeth her hands to the spindle, and her hands hold the distaff.
Proverbs 31:13, 19

Making Cloth

Today many people buy their clothes already made to fit them. Sometimes people make clothes from cloth that they buy in a store. Many years ago, people made their own clothes. They also made their own cloth.

Breaking flax to make thread

Most families made cloth from sheep's wool or from a plant called flax. If they wanted to make cloth from wool, they first had to shear, or cut, the wool from the sheep. Do you think they did this in the winter or the summer?

After it was cut, the wool had to be combed until it was soft and fluffy. Then the fluffy wool was spun into thread with a huge spinning wheel. It took practice to make fine, even thread with the big wheel. Once the thread was washed and dried, it was ready to weave into cloth. Would you like to make your own cloth?

Trouble in Boston

By the early fall of 1768, King George was tired of the colonists' disobedience. He thought of himself as their father. And he knew all fathers must be firm. So he sent his soldiers to the colonies. The soldiers would scare the colonists into doing what he said to do.

King George did not have much money to pay his soldiers. And he had not gotten much money by taxing the colonists. Why would this be a problem to the king? He could not afford to send soldiers to every colony. He had to choose the one best place to send his soldiers.

Where do you think King George sent the soldiers? The Massachusetts Colony had been the most disobedient of all the colonies. And the city of Boston had been the most trouble of all. That is where the soldiers went.

Do you think the people in Boston were scared of the soldiers? They were not. Do you think they decided to obey the king? They did not. They still would not pay the tax. They knew that King George would make more tax laws if they agreed to pay this tax.

The people of Boston did not like having the soldiers in their city. They did not like to have them camping on their pastureland. They did not like their drilling and making noise on Sundays. And they did not like their drinking and playing cards any day.

Many soldiers came to Boston. How many soldiers do you think King George sent? He sent four thousand men. Soon there was one soldier for every four colonists in Boston.

Boston in 1775

Colonists | Soldiers

The Boston Massacre

The soldiers, or *redcoats,* stayed in Boston a long time. The longer they stayed, the angrier the colonists got. Then an awful thing happened. A group of colonists fought with some soldiers. Five colonists died. What do you think happened then?

Men in Boston called this sad fight the *Boston Massacre.* They wrote letters to newspapers. They made pictures to put in the newspapers. They said and did things to make the other colonists angry with England and King George.

Samuel Adams

(1722-1803)

Samuel Adams was born in Boston in 1722. He grew up in a *middle-class* family. His parents were neither very poor nor very rich.

After Samuel finished college, he tried to set up a business in Boston. But Sam Adams was not a good businessman. He could not remember things he needed to do. He was always late for appointments. And he did not dress carefully. He often looked as if he had fallen out of a dirty ragbag.

Sam Adams could do one thing well. He could write. He wrote letters to the newspapers in Boston. Every week the newspapers printed what he wrote. The letters reminded the people of the taxes the king made them pay. Samuel Adams helped prepare the people to fight for their freedom.

A Huge Tea Party

In 1773 King George tried again to tax the colonies. He still wanted to tax tea. He knew that the people in the colonies liked to drink tea.

King George knew it would be hard to get the people to pay the tax. So he made a plan. The tea would be cheaper than any other tea they could buy, even with the tax! He made his plan work by letting only one company sell tea to the colonies.

Do you think his plan fooled the colonists? The colonists could not be fooled. They still would not pay a tax that they had not voted for.

King George went ahead with his plan. He picked men to sell the tea in each colony. The colonists tried to get these men to send the tea back to England. Some of the king's men agreed to send the tea back. But some did not. They wanted money for selling the tea. And they were afraid of the king.

The king's men in Boston would not send the tea back to England. So the colonists made their own plan. They would not let the king's men take the tea off the ships. The ships' captains did not know what to do. What would you have done?

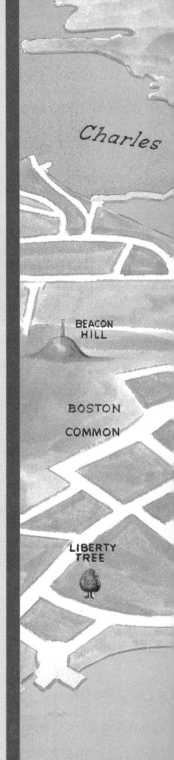

River

Mill Pond

OLD NORTH
CHURCH

FANEUIL
HALL

CUSTOM
HOUSE

BOSTON

Long   Wharfe

TOWN HOUSE

MAIN GUARD
HOUSE

HARBOUR

N

OLD SOUTH
MEETING HOUSE

GRAY'S ROPEWALK

Boston Harbor
December 16, 1773

A few hours before midnight

The men used charcoal, soot, and burned cork to make their faces dark. They wore clothing made from deerskin and put woven blankets over their shoulders. For many years after, no one knew exactly who these men were.

About one hundred men boarded the three tea ships. They took two hours to dump all the tea.

The men broke open 342 wooden crates of tea. They dumped all the tea into the sea.

A big crowd gathered on the docks to watch. No one spoke a word while the "Indians" worked.

When the men finished their work, they got brooms from the sailors. They swept the decks clean before they left.

Some colonists knew what to do. They dressed up as Mohawk Indians. They went onto the tea ships. They took every crate of tea and dumped it into the water. They called it the *Boston Tea Party.*

Do you think King George liked the Boston Tea Party? He did not. He sent more soldiers to Boston. And he made a new law for that city. No more ships could come into Boston. No ships could leave Boston.

King George's new laws made the colonists angry. So the colonists made another plan. They gathered guns and other weapons. Why do you think they did that? They wanted to be ready to fight. They were ready for a war with England.

Plead my cause, O Lord, with them that strive with me: fight against them that fight against me.

Psalm 35:1

To Have a Tea Party

1. Get a tablecloth, a vase with flowers, two teapots, some tea bags, napkins, cups, spoons, plates, sugar, a lemon, and some crackers or cookies.

2. Put the cloth and the vase on the table. Then set the napkins, dishes, spoons, sugar, lemon, and crackers or cookies on the cloth.

3. Ask your teacher to boil water and pour it into the teapots.

4. Choose someone to pour the tea. Be sure all the guests are served. The colonists had tea every afternoon. Would you like to have a tea party every afternoon?

10
Freedom

General Thomas Gage was worried. He was in charge of the king's soldiers in Boston. The king wanted him to make the colonists behave. But the colonists were gathering guns. They wanted to fight a war. What could General Gage do?

King George told him what to do. "Send my soldiers to find the guns!" he said.

The War Begins

Late in the night, seven hundred soldiers left Boston. They did not want the colonists to know what they were doing. Do you know where they were going? They were marching to Concord. They wanted to surprise the colonists there. Then they could take the guns, and the colonists could not fight.

Paul Revere
(1735-1818)

Paul Revere was one of the busiest men in Boston. He ran a silversmith shop his father had built. He made false teeth. And he made pictures to show to others. This is one of his best-known pictures. It shows the Boston Massacre.

Paul had other things to keep him busy too. But these things were secret. If the redcoats had caught him, they might have killed him. He joined a group of men who wanted freedom for the colonies. He carried letters to other cities. He helped the men learn secrets about the redcoats. He found guns to fight the redcoats with.

One message Paul carried was not written in a letter, but it was very important. He told the colonists that the redcoats were coming. They wanted to take the guns and bullets the colonists had hidden. Do you think the redcoats found the guns?

Lexington, Massachusetts
April 19, 1775

Just after dawn

Seventy men waited on the street. They had come from their homes while it was still dark. Paul Revere had told them that the king's soldiers were coming.

The men did not plan to fight. But they wanted to protect their town.

Soldiers appeared at the other end of the field. They told the men to put down their guns. They wanted the men to go home.

No one knows who fired his gun first. But that one shot began a long war.

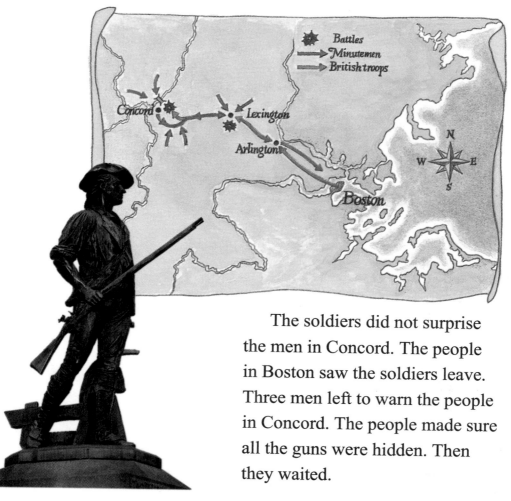

The soldiers did not surprise the men in Concord. The people in Boston saw the soldiers leave. Three men left to warn the people in Concord. The people made sure all the guns were hidden. Then they waited.

Men from other towns came to help too. They had promised to be ready to fight at any minute. Do you know what these men were called? They were *minutemen*.

The minutemen were not trained to fight. They did not dress like soldiers. Do you think they could beat the king's soldiers? They did. They chased them all the way back to Boston.

War in the Northern Colonies

Most colonists had not really meant to start a war with England. They tried to talk to King George. They asked him to treat them fairly. But he would not listen. He made laws that hurt them. He sent his redcoats to fight them.

Men from each colony met in Philadelphia. They wanted to make an American army. Each colony would send money to pay for the army. Each colony would send minutemen to fight. Together they could beat King George and his redcoats.

"We need someone to lead our army," they said. Do you know whom they chose? They picked a man who had been to war before. He was a hero.

They chose George Washington.

George Washington rode his horse to Boston. The men were glad to have a leader. They called him *General* Washington. The general would know what to do next.

The Americans waited. They dug trenches. They pointed their big guns, called *cannons,* at Boston. Would the redcoats try to fight again?

When the redcoats saw the cannons, they knew they had to leave Boston. They could not win a fight, or *battle,* against guns like that. So the redcoat general told his men to sail away from Boston on their ships. Soon no redcoats were left in Boston. Do you think that ended the war? The war was not over yet.

"We Are Free"

The battle along the road to Concord was the first battle of the colonists' *War for Independence*. *Independence* means "freedom." The colonists wanted the freedom to make their own laws. They wanted to be free from an unfair king.

The men met again in Philadelphia. They picked a man to write down the things they believed. Thomas Jefferson worked hard. He remembered the things that King George had done. He thought about what freedom meant. He wrote these things on paper. Then he showed the paper to the other men.

The men agreed with what Jefferson had written. They signed their names on the paper on July 4, 1776. Later they read it to the people in Philadelphia. The men called the words on the paper the *Declaration of Independence*. The words told everyone that the people in America were not colonists anymore. They were Americans. They would fight for their freedom.

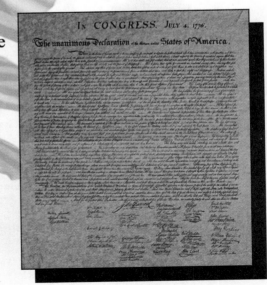

To Write Fancy

1. Get your Notebook page, a blank piece of paper, a ruler, and a pencil.

2. Find the letters that spell your name on the Notebook page. Then draw a straight line on the piece of paper. Trace the letters of your name on the paper. Use the line you drew to keep them straight.

3. Add some fancy lines or swirls to the letters or beneath your name. Practice writing your name that way two or three times. Would you like to write that way all the time?

Alexander

Alexander

Examples of signatures on the Declaration of Independence

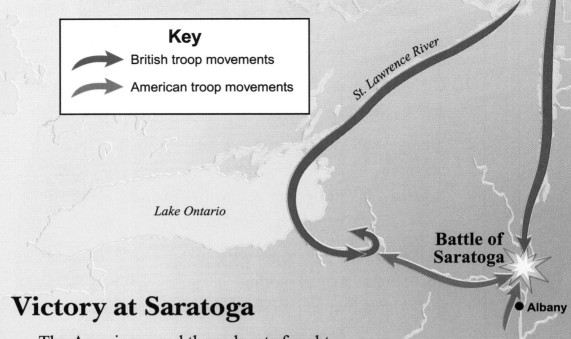

St. Lawrence River

Lake Ontario

Battle of Saratoga

● Albany

Victory at Saratoga

The Americans and the redcoats fought many more times. The Americans won a few times. The redcoats won more often. But the Americans would not give up.

Then parts of the two armies fought a battle in the woods of New York. It was a terrible battle that lasted many days. The Americans circled the redcoats. They could not escape. Finally, the redcoats gave up. The Americans captured almost six thousand of the king's men.

Winning at Saratoga was important for the Americans. It gave people hope. Now they believed that they could win the war. And other countries thought so too. France and Spain told the Americans that they would help them to fight the redcoats.

Benedict Arnold
(1741-1801)

Benedict Arnold was a good leader. Men liked to follow him into battle. He knew what to do to win. He was one of the leaders at the big battle in New York. Without his brave leading and hard work, the Americans might not have won that battle.

But Arnold was a proud man. Winning battles for his country was not enough for him. He wanted everyone to know how smart he was. And he was greedy. The American army could not pay him much money. He wanted more.

Arnold made a plan. He would find a way to get money from the redcoats. He told the redcoats secrets. He promised to let them have an American fort if they paid him money. "Now the redcoats will know how smart I am," he thought. "And the Americans will be sorry they did not pay me more."

General Washington found out about the plan. He was angry. The American people were angry. Benedict Arnold had been a hero. But today we do not think about the good things he did. We remember only that he turned against his country and the people who had been his friends. We call him a *traitor.*

> *A man's pride shall bring him low: but honour shall uphold the humble in spirit.*
> Proverbs 29:23

Valley Forge
January 1778

A cold wind blew across the winter camp of the American army. The gray-white clouds promised to bring yet another *blizzard,* or snowstorm.

More than one thousand log cabins filled the clearing. Each cabin was fourteen feet wide and sixteen feet long. Twelve men lived in each small cabin.

Most men did not have blankets or warm clothes. Many men did not even have shoes. They wrapped their cold feet in rags to keep them warm.

The men ate a kind of bread made from flour and water for every meal. The redcoats had bought or stolen all the animals and other food from the farmers near the camp.

The redcoats thought all the Americans would die at this camp. But they did not all die. They were ready to fight again in the spring.

The Americans who left Valley Forge were strong. They were ready to fight again. One man helped to make them ready. But that man was not an American. Ben Franklin, visiting in France, had sent him. He was not French, either. Baron von Steuben came from Prussia. He had fought in the army of Frederick the Great.

Baron von Steuben taught the men to march. He taught them to turn at the same time. He taught them to load their guns quickly and to use a weapon called a *bayonet*. He was a good *drillmaster*, or teacher.

The Baron did not speak English. His helpers told him the words to say. When the men did the right thing, he said, *"Ach, gut! Sehr gut!"* What do you think those words mean?

To March like a Soldier

1. You will be the soldier. Your teacher will be the drillmaster. You will need no other materials.

2. Listen carefully to your drillmaster. Do what you are told to do. Practice a salute if you are asked to. Be careful not to run into any other soldiers.

3. What things would a real soldier carry that you do not have? Would you like to be a real soldier? Why do soldiers have to learn how to march?

Heroes and Heroines

General Washington was proud of his men. They had worked hard during the long winter at Valley Forge. Now that it was spring, the men were ready to leave that camp. The redcoats were leaving their winter camp too. They were going to New York City.

The general had a plan. He wanted to attack the redcoats while they were marching to New York. If the Americans could catch up with the redcoats, they could win a battle. It was a good plan.

One of the American army leaders did not like the plan. He did not want to fight. He was afraid of losing the battle. So he told his men to stop fighting. The men ran. Then they saw General Washington. He was not running. The men stopped and fought the redcoats.

Mary "Molly Pitcher" Hays
(1754?-1832)

The sun was hot that early summer day. Mary wished she could rest in the shade. But the men on the battlefield needed her. They called her "Molly Pitcher" because she used a pitcher to bring them water.

As Molly carried the water to the men fighting beside her husband, she saw men running away from the battle. "Where are you going?" she asked.

"General Lee told us to stop fighting," they called out.

"No!" said Molly. "We can't stop!" Do you know what she did then? She helped to fire the cannon the men had left.

General Washington saw Molly firing the cannon. He said, "That is a very brave young lady. I am proud of what she did. I want everyone to know about it." He made Molly a sergeant in the army.

War in the Southern Colonies

The war was not going the way King George and his soldiers had thought it would. They had won a few battles, but the Americans would not stop fighting. After four years of war, the redcoats knew they needed another plan.

The redcoat general thought, "It will be easier to fight in the South. More Tories live in the South. They will come to fight with us. They will help us beat the Americans."

Who were these *Tories* that lived in the southern colonies? Tories were colonists who were loyal to the king. They hoped the redcoats would win the war. They even fought beside the redcoats against other colonists.

The redcoats sailed to Charleston. The ships pointed their cannon at the city. Some soldiers went to the land and dug trenches. Do you remember when a thing like this happened before? That time, the Americans made the redcoats leave Boston. This time, the redcoats made the Americans leave.

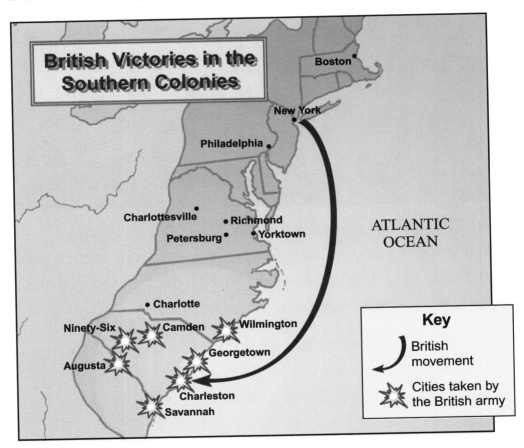

After they won at Charleston, the redcoats won many more battles. The Tories were happy. The redcoats were happy. They said, "This was a good idea. We will win the war now."

Writing Songs

Have you ever written a song? You do not have to be known as a songwriter to write a good song. If someone asked you to write a song, what would you write about?

People write songs about things they know. Sometimes people write songs for a celebration or to tell about a thing that happened. Sometimes people write a song to make fun of something. "Yankee Doodle" was such a song. An English army doctor wrote the song. He had seen the colonists' army. He thought the soldiers looked silly.

During the war, the redcoats sang the song and laughed at the American army. Do you think it made the Americans angry? It did not. They liked the song. Soon they started singing it too. "Yankee Doodle" is still a favorite song of Americans.

Yankee Doodle went to town A-riding on his po-ny He stuck a fea-ther in his cap and called it mac-a-ro-ni Yan-kee Doo-dle keep it up

But winning the war was not so easy as the redcoats had thought. The Americans did not have a big army in the South. So small groups of men attacked the redcoats. They kept the attacks secret. Each time, the redcoats were surprised. They could not catch the Americans.

By now, the redcoats were tired. They had fought the Americans for six years. The redcoat general led his men to a small town. They would rest there for the winter. They did not know that more Americans were on their way.

Soon the Americans got to that small town, called Yorktown. Their friends, the French, sailed in ships nearby. Black Americans and white Americans waited near the town. Friends from many countries waited beside them. They had trapped the redcoats. Would the war be over?

11
What
People Wore

Everyday Clothes
of Plymouth Plantation

Do you think that everyone dressed alike in Plymouth Plantation? Do you think the soldiers in George Washington's army all wore the same kind of uniform? Although the clothes of any time are alike in most ways, there are many differences.

Clothes that people wear can tell a great deal about how they live. If you see someone dressed like the woman in the picture, what would you think she does?

The life is more than meat, and the body is more than raiment.

Luke 12:23

Long ago the clothes people wore showed how much money they had, what work they did, where they came from, and sometimes even what they thought was important in life.

Here are drawings of a Separatist man and woman. Does anything surprise you about the pictures? What colors are their clothes? What do you think the clothes were made of?

Do you see any buttons on the Separatists' clothes? What kind of fasteners do you see? Do you think they lived where it is warm or cold much of the time? Why do you say so?

Separatists and Puritans liked nice-looking clothes. But they thought it was wrong to dress as though they had more money than they did. Some of them thought that it was not right to wear buttons and really bright colors.

They thought clothes should keep a person warm and help him do his work. They chose wool and other plain cloth for their clothes. What do the Separatists' clothes tell you about the Separatists? They wanted to please God with how they dressed.

What would make you think Separatists were hard working? What would make you think they wanted to live simple lives? What might the man in the picture do for a living? Why does the woman wear an apron?

Clothes, Rich and Plain

How do you think Plymouth children dressed? They did not have play clothes as you might think. They wore clothes that looked just like their parents' clothes. The only difference was that the children's clothes were smaller, of course, and sometimes more colorful.

Both adults and children usually had special Sunday clothes. Why do you think that was so? They thought going to church was important; they wanted to show that they thought so by not wearing work clothes.

Now look at the picture of the man and woman on this page. They lived at the same time as the Separatists. But they were not Separatists. They were rich people in England.

How are their clothes the same as the Separatists'? How are they different? What do you think their clothes tell about them? Do you think they worked hard?

Their clothes were made of velvets and satins. Do you think such cloth cost more or less than wool? Why do you think their clothes were fancy?

Look at the dress-up clothes in this picture. Do you think the people are Separatists? Why do you say so? How are the mother and child dressed alike? Do you think the people are poor or wealthy?

Clothes in Colonial Times

People who lived in the American colonies when George Washington did dressed another way. How had clothes changed in one hundred years?

Do you think the people in the drawing were rich or poor? What color seems to have been popular in that time? Why do you think that was so? Would you like to wear these kinds of clothes?

Soldiers' Clothes

During the Revolutionary War, the soldiers in George Washington's army wore many different kinds of uniforms. Some soldiers just wore their everyday clothes.

Look at the picture of the soldier from Virginia. He fought far away from the towns. He often stayed in the woods. Do any of his clothes make you think of Indian clothes?

He wore leggings and *moccasins,* an Indian shoe. He carried an Indian pouch. What do his clothes tell you about him?

Here is a soldier from Rhode Island. How were his clothes like the soldier's from Virginia? How were they different?

Why do you think he wore the big belts crossed on his chest? They held up his sword and bullet case. The gun he carried is called a *musket*. It was a very heavy gun. It weighed as much as a collie dog or twenty of these books.

Most of the soldiers who wore this uniform were black. They fought in one of the most important battles. They saw the British lose the war and give up.

This is one of King George's soldiers. How was his uniform different from the Americans' uniforms? Can you see why the Americans called these soldiers *redcoats?*

The case on his belt held bullets. What do you think the *GR* on it and on the gun in the photo means?

It stands for King George. *George Rex* means "George the King."

To Make a Colonial Hat

1. *Boys*—Get four black hat pieces and some tape.
   Girls—Get a circle of fabric two feet across and a yard of thin ribbon.

2. Put your hat together. Your teacher will show you how.

3. Try on your Colonial hat. Would you like to wear a hat all the time?

Wearing Wigs

In the days of George Washington, many men wore wigs. Do you think they wore wigs because they were bald? Not always. Most wore wigs because it was the fashion.

Important men wore wigs. Judges and leaders wore them. George Washington often wore one.

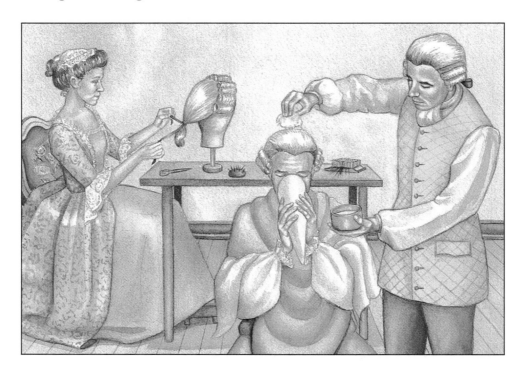

The men powdered their wigs white. They pulled the hair back into a low ponytail. They tied the ponytail with a black ribbon. The wigs were heavy and hot. Do you wear anything just because it is the fashion?

Later Clothes

One hundred years after George Washington lived, the clothes looked like this. How are these clothes different from Colonial clothes? How are they different from Plymouth clothes?

In some ways the clothes stayed the same from Plymouth times to Colonial times to the time of these clothes. The women all wore long skirts. The men wore pants with a jacket or vest.

What do you notice about the children's clothes here? The children have clothes that are not exactly like the adults' clothes.

Would you like to dress like this?

175

Look at the people on this page. They are in order the way they would have come in history. Can you tell which is the Separatist? Which lived in George Washington's day? Where would you like to be on this line?

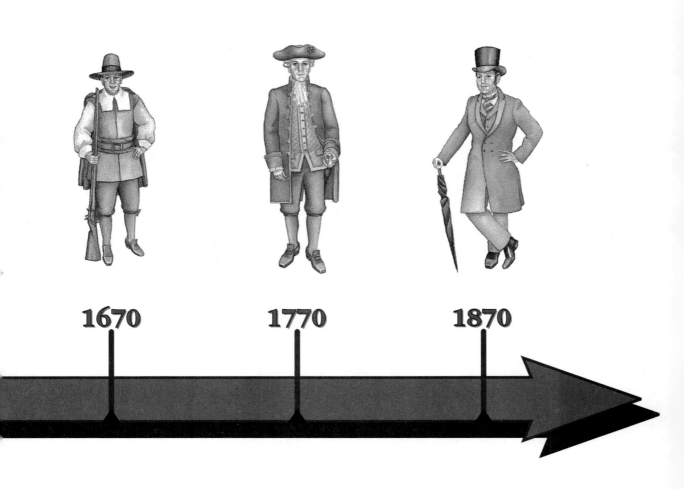

1670   1770   1870

People wear clothes to keep warm. They wear clothes to be modest. They wear clothes to help in their work. They wear clothes to look good. Which of these reasons are most important to you?

Why do you think the clothes we wear today are so different from clothes in the past? Partly our clothes show that our houses are warmer in the winter. The Separatists had only fireplaces to keep them warm. They wore heavy clothes even inside.

Partly our clothes are different because ideas about what is right and wrong have changed. Few women wear floor-length skirts anymore. People used to think it was wrong for a woman's ankles to show.

We still wear clothes to keep warm. Some people still wear special clothes because of the work they do. Nurses do; police officers do. People of all times have chosen their clothes for the same reasons.

Look at your clothes. What do they say about you?

12
Starting
a Country

A New Country

Late in the night, a rider galloped from Yorktown to Philadelphia. He was sick with a fever, and he had ridden for two days. But he did not stop to rest. He rode right to the houses and woke up the leaders of the city. "The redcoats have given up!" he said.

The leaders said, "Ring the bells! Let the people know they are free!" The bells of Philadelphia chimed out. America was now a country by itself. It was a new nation.

Let all things be done decently and in order.
I Corinthians 14:40

Now the time had come to decide how to run a new country. The leaders of all the colonies had many different ideas. Suppose you had been a leader then. Would you have wanted to get another king? Would you have wanted to be the ruler of the new nation?

Twelve of the colonies sent men to Philadelphia. The men had to make up rules to help the new country. The men had to make the thirteen colonies into one nation. They met in the State House at Philadelphia. Today we call the building *Independence Hall.*

Other countries of the world waited to see what would happen. Spain and England hoped that the country would fall apart. They were ready to take land from the Americans if the Americans could not run their country.

The summer was hot. A lot of big, biting flies swarmed around the town. The men in the State House argued with each other.

"No," said one, "all the states should have the same number of votes."

"No," said another, "that is not fair. Small states should not have as many votes as big states. States with more people should have more votes."

What would you have said? Suppose you and your friends were making rules for all your families to go by. Would you think that families with many children should have more votes than families with one or two children?

The man in charge of the meeting was George Washington. He sat quietly. He listened to all that the men said. He did not give his ideas. He was there to keep order. Another man who sat and listened was Benjamin Franklin. Mr. Franklin was now eighty-one years old.

Day after day the men talked about how the new government should be run. They took votes on the different ideas. Some days it must have been hard to think. It was hot. Some men waved fans in front of their faces. Flies buzzed outside.

The men did not meet on the Fourth of July. Why do you think they took that day off? The city of Philadelphia had a celebration. The bells rang, and fireworks lit the sky. At night, every house had candles in all the windows.

The Great Compromise

The next day all the men met in the State House again. They began to talk over the rules again. Benjamin Franklin shook his head. George Washington looked sad. People began to think that the men would not come up with a plan that would make everybody happy.

No one could agree about the number of votes that states should have. Then at last they came up with a compromise. A *compromise* is an agreement that is not exactly what either side wants but is good enough for both sides to like.

A man read a report. He said, "Since we cannot decide whether big states should have more votes than small states, let's have both. In the *Senate,* every state will have two votes. In the *House,* every state will have one vote for every forty thousand people who live in that state."

The *Senate* and the *House* are the two parts of our government that make our laws. Both parts must agree that an idea is good before it can be a law.

Everyone started talking to everyone else. The voices got loud. Washington at last called for a vote. He knew that the whole future of the country might rest on that vote.

Philadelphia
July 16, 1787

The State House

The "compromise" was up for a vote.

The votes were counted.

| YES | Delaware, Maryland, Connecticut, New Jersey, and North Carolina said yes. |

| NO | Virginia, Pennsylvania, South Carolina, and Georgia said no. |

Did the idea pass?
The compromise passed.

Now the Congress has two parts. Both parts, or houses, meet in this building in Washington, D.C.

Now the men in Philadelphia had another problem.

One man said, "Who should lead the government?"

Another said, "We do not want another king!"

Everyone in the room cheered at that. America did not want a king. The colonies had fought hard to get rid of the last king. The men decided to call the leader of the new nation *president.*

We have had more than forty presidents in our country. This is the place where the president works. Have you ever been to the White House?

Our First President

Everybody knew who the first president would be. It would be George Washington. He had led the American army in the war. He had been the leader at Philadelphia. He would make a good president for the new nation.

The men finally had rules written that they wanted to show the people of America. They called the rules the *Constitution*. Printers made copies of the Constitution. Newspapers printed the rules and told what they meant. Everyone had a chance to read about the Constitution. Why was that important?

The people in the thirteen states talked about the new rules. They decided what they thought of the rules. They voted on them. When the people voted, most of them said the new laws were good. The Constitution became the law for our country.

What do you think the people who did not like the Constitution did? Do you think they got angry because most people voted for the Constitution? No, they did not. They said that the vote had been fair and that they had lost. But they said they wanted to be good citizens of the new country. They said that they would live by the rules that everyone had voted on.

What do you think it means to be a good citizen? It means that you pay attention to the laws that the government makes. It means that you vote when you are old enough. It means you pay taxes. It means you live by the rules that are made. Why is it important for a country to have rules? Why does a family need rules?

George Washington
(1732-1799)

When he was a little boy, George Washington probably never thought that he would become famous. He grew up learning to farm. Do you think he guessed that he would become the first president of a brand-new country?

George Washington was a quiet man. But he knew how to be strong. His courage had kept the poor army together in bad times. He had helped the soldiers stay through the hard winter at Valley Forge. He always thought of his country first.

He was at Philadelphia, sitting in the State House every day. The meetings went better because he came. The men there liked Washington. They did not fight if he asked them not to. They tried to behave as he did. He was calm and kind.

The Constitution

The Constitution is an important paper in our history. It makes the United States special. It gives every American the same rights as every other American. We should be proud of our country and its Constitution.

Can you think of another important paper in our history? The Declaration of Independence is important. Why was it important? Do you remember who wrote it?

The Constitution was signed by the men who had come from the twelve colonies. It was an honor to sign such a great paper. Important papers in our country have something special on them. They have a stamp called the *Great Seal.* You can see the Great Seal on the back of a one-dollar bill. Both sides of the seal are shown.

To Make a Great Seal

1. Get your Notebook; some brown, blue, red, and yellow construction paper; some crayons; some stars; some scissors; and some glue.

2. Use the patterns in your Notebook. Cut out the pieces from the construction paper as your teacher tells you. Use the crayons to color the beak, the shield, the olive branch, the leg feathers, and the claws.

3. Glue the papers together to make a Great Seal. Draw the arrows and the olive branch. Do you know what the Great Seal stands for? Tell someone about it.

What do you think the other countries thought about the United States? They were surprised that a new country could make such a good government. They had not believed that people who were used to war could calmly make laws.

The United States took its place among the nations of the world. The leaders made peace with England. Soon the two nations were buying and selling goods with each other. The new country was already becoming a powerful nation.

Many people believe that God blessed America. He had wise, just leaders ready when they were needed. He honored people who wanted to live where they could worship Him freely.

Blessed is the nation whose God is the Lord.
Psalm 33:12

It is our duty to keep the freedom that the Constitution talks about. We must remember all that went into the making of this mighty country of ours. And we must never forget that doing right is what makes a country strong.

Resource Treasury

Signs of Freedom

Liberty Bell

The bell we know as the Liberty Bell was first called the State House Bell.

It rang at important times. It rang at the reading of the Declaration of Independence. It rang when George Washington became the first president.

It rang the last time in 1835. Then the crack in it became too big.

Today it has its own house in Philadelphia. You can go there and touch it.

The big bell stands for freedom. Have you ever seen it?

Independence Hall

This old building looks small, but it is a big place in our history.

The Declaration of Independence was written here.

In this hall fifty-five men wrote the Constitution of the United States.

It has been called the "cradle of liberty." Why do you think it is called that? Our freedom began here.

Flags of the United States

Every colony had a different flag before the War for Independence.

In 1776, the colonies had one flag. It looked like this one.

After the colonies declared themselves no longer a part of England, the flag looked like this one.

Now our flag looks like this one.

Why does it have thirteen stripes? It has a stripe for each colony. Why does it have fifty stars? It has a star for each state.

The Declaration of Independence

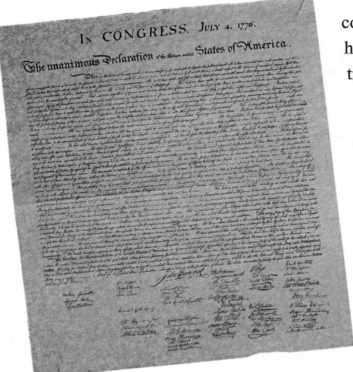

The leaders of the colonies wrote down how King George had treated them badly.

They wrote down how they had tried to tell the king to stop.

They wrote down the reasons the colonies had to be free from the king.

The paper they wrote is called the Declaration of Independence.

The Declaration of Independence is our first sign of freedom.

Special Days

The First Fourth of July

July 4, 1777
Philadelphia

The State House Bell rang. All the other bells rang too. Much later the State House Bell cracked and became known as the "Liberty Bell."

Ships in the harbor fired their guns.

Fireworks lit the sky.

Almost every house had candles in all the windows.

Soldiers and horses paraded through the streets.

The Fourth of July Now

Many towns have parades.

Some places have fireworks.

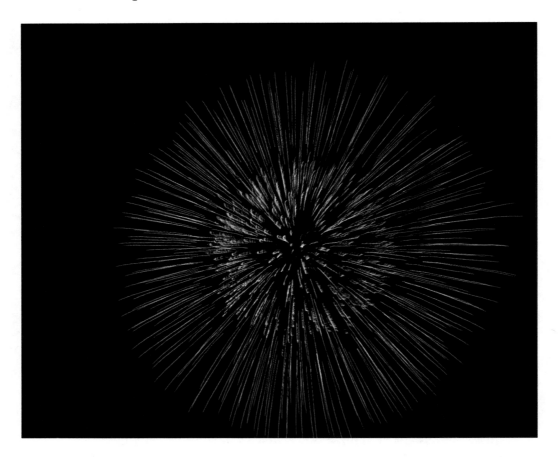

What do you do on the Fourth of July? We should always remember to thank the Lord for our country.

Washington's Birthday

The people of the United States loved President Washington. On his birthday they fired guns and rang bells and held parades. The president came out to greet all the people.

Today we remember our first president on Presidents' Day.

Flag Day

June 14 is Flag Day.

American flags fly from many places on that day.

We celebrate Flag Day on June 14 for an important reason. On June 14, 1777, the new United States decided how its flag should look.

The flag was to have thirteen stars and thirteen stripes.

Now the flag has thirteen stripes and fifty stars. Why do you think it does not have fifty stripes?

Traditions

John Smith and Pocahontas

Captain John Smith told a story. He said, "I was taken by the Indians. They were going to kill me. Then the chief's young daughter came. She begged her father not to kill me. Pocahontas saved my life." No one knows for sure that this story is true.

A German Christmas Custom

No one knows who first used a tree at Christmas. But the German people were the first to decorate a tree at Christmas. They put stars, toys, and candy on the tree. They put candles on it too. The tree reminds us of faithfulness. It is always green. The candles make us think of Jesus, the Light of the World.

Betsy Ross

Betsy Ross lived in Philadelphia. She lived there during the War for Independence.

Betsy was a flag maker. Some people think she may have made the first flag for America. How many stars and stripes would this flag have had?

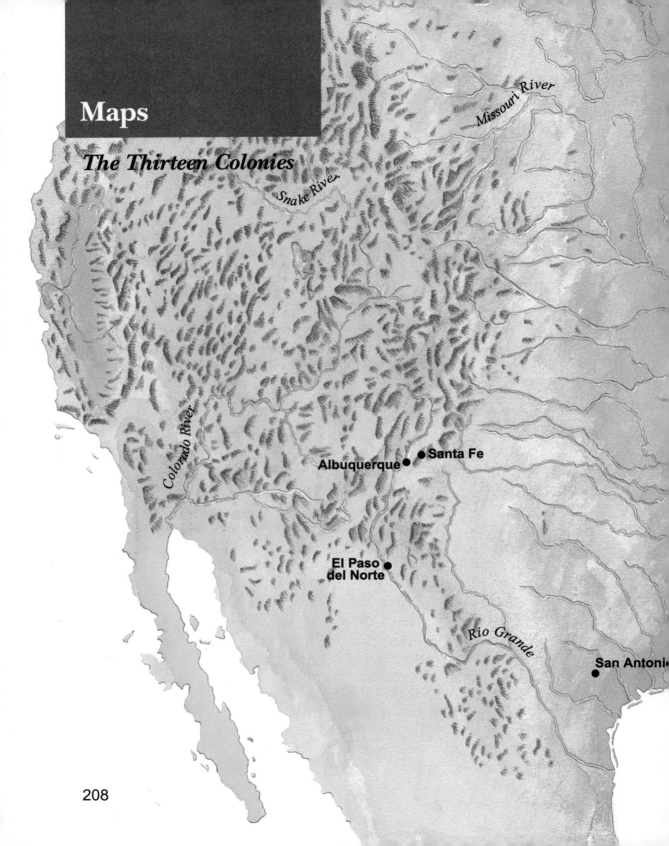

Maps

The Thirteen Colonies

Lake Superior

Sault Ste. Marie

Quebec

Massachusetts

Montreal

St. Lawrence River

New York

New Hampshire

Lake Michigan

Lake Huron

L. Ontario

Fort Niagara

Lake Erie

Albany

Hartford

Boston

Rhode Island

Connecticut

New York

Philadelphia

Pennsylvania

Missouri River

Ohio River

Virginia

Baltimore

New Jersey

Delaware

St. Louis

Richmond

Williamsburg

Maryland

North Carolina

New Bern

Arkansas Post

South Carolina

Wilmington

Mississippi River

Georgia

Savannah

Mobile

Pensacola

New Orleans

St. Augustine

N

W   E

S

209

The United States Today

Washington

Oregon

Montana

North Dakota

Idaho

South Dakota

Wyoming

Nevada

Nebraska

Utah

Colorado

California

Kansas

Arizona

Oklahoma

New Mexico

Texas

Alaska

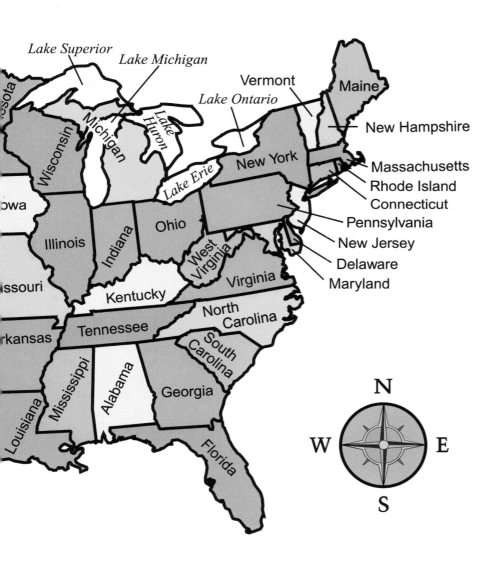

Lake Superior

Lake Michigan

Lake Ontario

Vermont

Maine

Lake
Huron

New Hampshire

Wisconsin

Michigan

Lake Erie

New York

Massachusetts

Rhode Island

Connecticut

owa

Ohio

Pennsylvania

Illinois

Indiana

New Jersey

West
Virginia

Delaware

ssouri

Kentucky

Virginia

Maryland

rkansas

Tennessee

North
Carolina

Mississippi

Alabama

South
Carolina

Louisiana

Georgia

Florida

N

W

E

S

Hawaii

Countries of the World

213

Geogloss

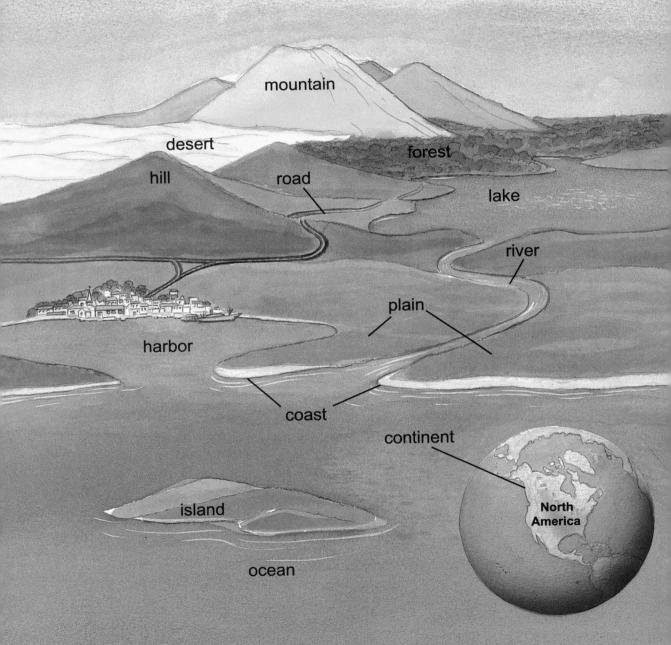

mountain

desert

forest

hill

road

lake

river

plain

harbor

coast

continent

North America

island

ocean

Glossary

address the writing on mail that tells where it is sent

apprentice *(ə-pren'tis)* one who works for another to learn a trade

blacksmith one who works with iron

Boston Massacre *(bô'stən mas'ə-kər)* a fight between colonists and redcoats in which five colonists died

Boston Tea Party the time colonists threw tea off British ships to show that they hated the tea tax

census *(sen'səs)* the government's counting of people

coat of arms a picture of objects that represent a family

colonist one who lives in a colony

colony a faraway place in which people settle

community a group of people living in the same place

compromise *(kom'prə-mīz')* an idea that is not exactly what either side wants but is good enough for both sides to like

Constitution a paper that gives the main laws of the United States

Declaration of Independence a paper that says the American colonies do not belong to King George

French and Indian Wars battles between France and England over American land

George Rex King George III of England

Great Seal the special stamp used by the United States on important papers

House of Representatives one of the two groups of people who make laws for the United States

independence freedom from rules and rulers that the people did not choose

Independence Hall a building in Philadelphia in which the Declaration of Independence and the Constitution were written

Jamestown the oldest English town in the colonies

laws rules by which nations and cities live

lending library a place where people can borrow books for free

limner *(lim′nər)* a ready-made painting on which an artist paints a customer's face; also, the artist who does such painting

Louis XV a king of France

Mayflower the ship that brought Separatists and others to the New World

minutemen colonists who promised to be ready in a minute to fight the redcoats

musket *(mus′kit)* a gun used by many in the War for Independence

pesthouses places for people who had nowhere else to go

population *(pop'yə-lā'shən)* all the people that live in one place

postal system *(pōst'əl sis'təm)* the part of the government that delivers the mail

president *(prez'i-dənt)* the leader of the United States

redcoats King George's soldiers

Senate *(sen'it)* one of the two groups of people who make laws for the United States

Separatist one who did not agree with the Puritans and their hope for correcting the Church of England

slaves people bought by others and made to work for no money when they did not want to

tax money governments make people pay

Thanksgiving Day a special day for giving thanks to God

Tory *(tôr'ē)* a colonist who believed King George was right

traitor *(trā'tər)* a person who leaves his friends to help his enemies

trencher *(tren'chər)* a large wooden plate

War for Independence the fight between the American colonists and King George's soldiers

Index

Photograph Credits

The following agencies and individuals have furnished materials to meet the photographic needs of this textbook. We wish to express our gratitude to them for their important contribution.

Suzanne R. Altizer
Architect of the Capitol
British Official Photograph
George Buckley
Chicago Association of Commerce and Industry
George R. Collins
Corel Corporation
Terry M. Davenport
Farm Bureau Management Corporation

Greenville Children's Hospital
Dwight Gustafson
Independence National Historical Park
Mardella Jones
Roland Knight
Library of Congress
Los Angeles Public Library
National Archives
National Cotton Council
National Park Service

New York State Commerce Department
Pocumtuck Valley Memorial Association
Wade K. Ramsey
The Bob Jones University Collection
United States Department of Agriculture (USDA)
Unusual Films
Dawn L. Watkins

Cover/Title Page
Dawn L. Watkins (all)

Chapter 1
Dawn L. Watkins 1; Suzanne R. Altizer 2 (top); USDA 2 (bottom); Corel Corporation 3, 5; Unusual Films 6, 10; Courtesy of Roland Knight, M.D. 13 (top); Courtesy of Greenville Children's Hospital 13 (bottom); The Bob Jones University Collection 14

Chapter 2
Dawn L. Watkins 15, 17 (both), 22 (bottom), 24, 25 (top); Farm Bureau Management Corporation 16, 25 (bottom); National Cotton Council 22 (top); Unusual Films 23, 30 (all); USDA 26; Library of Congress 28; Corel Corporation 29

Chapter 3
Dawn L. Watkins 31; Corel Corporation 35; Unusual Films 48

Chapter 4
Courtesy of George Buckley 49; Dawn L. Watkins 52, 58; Unusual Films 54, 64 (all)

Chapter 5
Dawn L. Watkins 65; Los Angeles Public Library 66 (top); Chicago Association of Commerce and Industry 66 (middle); Courtesy of Mardella Jones 66 (bottom); Unusual Films 69 (both); Corel Corporation 72; The Bob Jones University Collection 74

Chapter 6
Courtesy of George Buckley 75; George R. Collins 76; Dawn L. Watkins 79, 80 (both), 82 (both), 83, 84, 85 (both), 89; Unusual Films 86, 90 (all)

Chapter 7
British Official Photograph 91; Dwight Gustafson 96; Unusual Films 97, 107, 108 (top); The Bob Jones University Collection 108 (bottom)

Chapter 8
Library of Congress 109, 121; Unusual Films 110, 114; Pocumtuck Valley Memorial Association 113; New York State Commerce Department 115; Dawn L. Watkins 122

Chapter 9
George R. Collins 123, 134 (top); Unusual Films 127; Dawn L. Watkins 130 (both); National Archives 134 (bottom); Library of Congress 135

Chapter 10
Architect of the Capitol 141; George R. Collins 144, 145; National Archives 146; Terry M. Davenport 148 (background); Unusual Films 148 (bottom), 154; Dawn L. Watkins 157

Chapter 11
Dawn L. Watkins 161, 172, 177 (all), 178; Unusual Films 162, 173

Chapter 12
George Buckley 179; George R. Collins 180, 181, 186; Architect of the Capitol 182; Wade K. Ramsey 187; Unusual Films 188, 191, 192, 194; Suzanne R. Altizer 189 (both)

Resource Treasury
National Park Service 195; Independence National Historical Park 196, 197; Unusual Films 200; George R. Collins 201; George Buckley 202, 207